CRACKING IT INTERVIEWS

Empowering Budding IT Professionals to Perform Outstandingly in Campus Placement Interviews

"We want that education by which character is formed, strength of mind is increased, the intellect is expanded, and by which one can stand on one's own feet..."

... **Swami Vivekananda**

"The meaning of education is to encourage in people a sense of self-introspection, the ability to grasp and to develop the capacity for constructive works..."

... **Dr. S. Radhakrishnan**

"Always surround yourself with the kind of people who can make you believe that you can do it..."

... **R. S. Salaria**

"Treat others the way you wish to be treated..."

... **R. S. Salaria**

"May the blessings of the almighty go with this book to one and all..."

... **R. S. Salaria**

CRACKING IT INTERVIEWS

Empowering Budding IT Professionals to Perform Outstandingly in Campus Placement Interviews

R. S. SALARIA

Alumnus of IIT, Delhi.
Certified Software Quality Professional, Govt. of India.
SUN Certified Programmer, SUN Microsystems, USA.
SUN Certified Trainer, SUN Microsystems, USA.

Former Head
Department of Computer Science & Engineering
Thapar University, Patiala

Professor & Head
Department of Computer Science & Engineering
Rayat-Bahra Institute of Engineering & Nano-Technology
Hoshiarpur (Punjab)

Assisted by
Anita Salaria

KHANNA BOOK PUBLISHING CO. (P) LTD.

Publisher of Engineering and Computer Books

4C/4344, Ansari Road, Darya Ganj, New Delhi-110002
Phone : 011-23244447-48 **Mobile:** +91-9910909320
E-mail : contact@khannabooks.com
Website : www.khannabooks.com

Dear Readers,

To prevent the piracy, this book is secured with HIGH SECURITY HOLOGRAM on the front title cover. In case you don't find the hologram on the front cover title, please write us to at contact@khannabooks.com or whatsapp us at +91-99109 09320 and avail special gift voucher for yourself.

Specimen of Hologram on front Cover title:

Moreover, there is a SPECIAL DISCOUNT COUPON for you with EVERY HOLOGRAM.

How to avail this SPECIAL DISCOUNT:

Step 1: Scratch the hologram
Step 2: Under the scratch area, your "coupon code" is available
Step 3: Logon to www.khannabooks.com
Step 4: Use your "coupon code" in the shopping cart and get your copy at a special discount
Step 5: Enjoy your reading!

Thanks,
Khanna Publishing House

Cracking IT Interviews
by **R. S. Salaria**

ISBN: 978-93-82609-96-4

To view complete list of books, please scan the QR Code:

Published by:
Khanna Book Publishing Co. (P) Ltd.
CIN: U22110DL1998PTC095547

Visit us at: www.khannabooks.com
Write us at: contact@khannabooks.com

Printed in Bharat.

Dedication

Our Dearest Parents,
Daughters Surbhi & Mehak,
Beloved Readers,

AND

Our Country Men/Women at Large.

My Slogan for My Fellow Citizens

India . . .

. . . is a Great Country

AND

Indians . . .

. . . are Outstanding.

Preface

It is a dream of every budding engineer to make it big in the corporate IT world. This book is designed to guide and empower the budding engineers to achieve their much cherished dream.

Since it is the interview process where the employability of the budding engineer is judged, therefore, keeping this aspect in mind, the first chapter is designed to guide the budding engineer to the most basic aspects of the interview process, and how meticulously they should plan and prepare for the interview.

Further, majority of the IT companies don't expect that the budding engineers should be well equipped with the advanced techniques/technologies, but must have strong foundation in the basics and concepts of the concerned subjects. In addition, they should be able to demonstrate the burning desire to excel and passion to learn. Keeping these aspects in mind, subsequent six chapters are designed to impart basic knowledge of the important topics through frequently asked questions in each topic.

I can assure you that any budding engineer, who can master about 70-75% questions covered in the books, can crack technical round of any IT company with a bang.

With a hope that this book will meet your expectations, I request you to send me your valuable feedback and suggestions at *rssalaraia@yahoo.com*, which will help me in tuning the book to your expectations.

Acknowledgments

It is my pleasure to take this opportunity to thank all those who helped me directly and indirectly in preparation of this book.

I thank my wife *Anita*, and daughters *Surbhi* and *Mehak*, for bearing with me during odd hours once again.

Finally, I must thank my publisher, Mr. Mukul Seth & Mr. Puneet Khanna for publishing this book.

Email : ***rssalaria@yahoo.com*** **. . . R. S. Salaria**

Word of Advice for Budding IT Professionals

My beloved students, I would like to remind you that we can categorize people as

People who watch the things happening,
People who look into how things are happening, and
People who make the things happen.

Now you are to find out where you fit-in and where you want to be.

I firmly believe that youth of our country is second to none, and this fact is recognized world wide.

Our honourable former president Late Dr. APJ Kalam (first and may be the last president known as *people's president*) has been saying at all the platform that in India there is no dearth of resources and talent, only thing we need to change is *the mindset* (we have to shed *chalta hai* attitude). He has set a vision for us to see India a developed country by 2020, and the basis for his vision is the talent of our youth.

Take some time to discover yourself and try to assess how much talent you possess. Utilize your period of study to harness that talent. I can assure you that you will have a great future.

I want to share a popular game with you which all of us used to play in our childhood. The game is of burning a peace of paper using a lens under the sun. When the lens and the paper are held stationery, it starts burning in a few seconds. However, if you keep moving either the paper or the lens, the paper will never burn. *Why it happens so?* The answer is simple – the light energy emitted by the sun is not focused. The same is with us. We have enough energy in ourselves, but we don't focus it, rather we waste it in meaningless acts. The next question arises is – *where to focus our energy?* The natural answer of this question should be – what you want to become in your life (that basically defines your goal). So you need to focus your entire energy on your goal, and surely you will achieve your goal.

I would also like to share with you a scene from the popular epic – *Mahabharta.* When Dronacharya, Guru of Pandvas, asked his disciples to aim at the eye of a sparrow hanged on a tree. All his disciples, except Arjuna, replied in a same manner – *Guru ji, we see a sparrow.* However, when the turn of Arjuna came, his reply was – *Guru ji, I see only the eye.* That is the kind of the focus you also need to develop in your life.

The next point is that when you have identified your goal, you need to identify the steps that you need to follow in order to accomplish your goal. Once the goal and the steps to accomplish your goal are identified, write them nicely on a piece of a paper and paste that paper at a place which you visit regularly. Whenever you will visit that place, the writing on the paper will remind you about your goal and what you have to do to achieve your goal.

The final word, you may set any goal for yourself and that may be of becoming a successful doctor, an engineer, an administrator or a businessman, but you must also try to be a *nice human being*. You know a nice human being is like a fruit of all seasons, and is welcome every where, anytime.

I believe, the basic mantra to become a nice human being is too simple and can be stated as

"Treat the others the way you want to be treated, in other words,
don't do anything with others which you wish
others shouldn't do with you."

Enjoy your student life and make best use of it . . .

Wish you good luck and a nice time ahead.

. . . R. S. Salaria

Table of Contents

Chapter 1

Introduction to Interview Process

1.1 INTRODUCTION

Interview is a process which can open many doors for you and it can close many doors for you too.

Therefore, an interview must not be taken casually; rather it must be meticulously planned followed by rigorous preparation. Though, there is no particular and fixed way to prepare for an interview still there are some important points that can be helpful in planning and preparing for the interview.

In this chapter, an attempt is made to guide you about the possible points that can be helpful in planning, preparation and finally cracking (conquering) the interview.

1.2 MAKE THE FIRST IMPRESSION

Note that the first impression and the last impression can make a lot of difference to you as well as the person(s) you are impressing upon, therefore, be careful and don't forget to make a good impression on both the occasions. First we will talk about the first impression.

Now a days, hidden cameras are placed in reception and waiting areas, from where your conduct is being monitored, starting from your arrival at the reception counter, your interaction with the receptionist, your interactions with other candidates, and your other activities and actions. This conduct of yours before you are called for interview, demonstrates volumes about your emotional maturity and your professional approach. Candidates who lack this attribute of personally are generally asked politely to leave with a false promise (sometimes) they will be called later on.

Therefore, take care of yourself and demonstrate through professionalism in your every act/action.

When you enter the interview room and by the time you reach to your hot seat, almost half of the interview is over. The interviewers (the persons in the interview panel) already have first impression of yours which can go in your favour or can go against you. You may be surprised, how?

Here it is important to note that the way you open the door and close the door after entering the interview room, reflects your etiquettes and your confidence. Closing the door gently and abruptly conveys a lot. It may show that are you calm person or a person in hurry?

The next thing they observe is the way you have dressed up yourself for the occasion. If you are asked to be in college/institute prescribed dress, then it is OK, otherwise the combination you wear speaks at a lot about your dressing sense, which reflects a lot about your personality. Further, you may be in college/institute prescribed dress or dress of your own choice; it should not appear to be untidy. For example, necktie should be properly tied; shirt should be properly inside the trouser, etc.

The next thing they observe in you is the confidence. You body language speaks a lot about you during the distance you travel from the entrance door to the hot seat. The position of your head, the position of your shoulders, the step sizes you take, and most importantly your facial expressions. Therefore, be careful about these aspects while you walk up to the hot seat. Position of your head should be straight and your face should be positioned towards the interviewers. Shoulders should be positioned straight so that your chest opens wide. Your step size during your walk should neither be too small nor be too long, and your walk should demonstrate that you are a clam and confident person not a person in a hurry. Finally, have a smile on your face that should reflect your preparedness for the occasion as well as your confidence.

The final thing that matters a lot is the way you greet the interviewers. It should be pleasant greetings such as “A very good Morning/Noon/Evening to all” depending on the timing of your call. After greeting, wait till you are offered the (hot) seat. After you occupy the hot seat, keep your file folder on the table in front of you, and keep your arms on your legs not on the table, and stay clam and confident till the interaction is initiated from the interviewers.

1.3 DURING THE INTERVIEW

During the interview, keep your clam and coolness, and demonstrate that you are a good listener. Listen to every question patiently, and if you are not able to understand the question properly, politely ask for its repeat, for example, say pardon sir/madam, can you repeat your question? Note that if you have not understood the question properly, your answer is going to be wavering, i.e., off the target. While you answer, maintain eye-to-eye contact with the interviewers. Note that maintaining eye-to-eye contact reflects that you are a confident person.

During the interview process, demonstrate that you are honest and straight forward person who is always ready to learn. If you are not sure about the answer, frankly say, I am not sure but I can try if you permit; and if you don't have the answer, frankly say, I am sorry sir/madam, but I will learn.

1.4 AFTER THE INTERVIEW – THE LAST IMPRESSION

Once your interview is over, the last question that may come up from the panel is – Do you have any question? Then you can get your doubts cleared about the company, if any. And if you find that no such question is coming from the interviewers, then you take the initiative and say – Sir/madam I have a question, if you permit. And then ask your question.

I am sure, if you have planned and prepared well for your interview, it must have gone your way.

But still, an interview can through up surprises because there is always an element of uncertainty in the interview. With your confidence, you can even handle those questions for which you have not even prepared.

Remember: More you know, less fear you have; less you know, you have only fear. Therefore, confidence only comes with knowledge.

Let us suppose that the interview had not gone your way (as you expected or the way you prepared), still you can force the interviewers to re-think about your candidature by following nice words before you leave your hot seat –

"Sir/Madam, I really enjoyed being interviewed by such enlightened and wonderful people in the panel, and this interview will remain etched in my memory for long, thank you very much!"

I am very sure that after you leave the room, the experts in the panel will re-think about your candidature again, and every member of the panel will be have a feeling that this candidate seems to be good, and today may not be his/her day, and you are likely to be re-called for another round of interview.

1.5 PLANNING AND PREPARING FOR THE INTERVIEW

In this section, we will take some aspects that will help us in planning and preparing for the interview.

1.6.1 Preparing Resume

Resume is very important document and it is the only tool with the potential employer to check your suitability/competence for the job, and therefore, writing a good resume for a job is the most important and perhaps the only tool to make a first impression on the potential employer.

Ensure the following points in your resume:

1. **Size:** Ensure that resume doesn't span more than two to three pages. No one likes to read lengthy articles on your achievements. They would prefer to get it from you in person.
2. **Format:** Ensure that resume should not have fuzzy look.
    - Use a standard and easily readable font consistently in the document.
    - Have proper and meaningful headings.
    - Italicize characters judiciously and avoid excessive colors.
    - Give the resume an overall professional look.
3. **Grammatical Errors:** Ensure that resume should not have any grammatical error.
4. **Contact Details:** Ensure that you have provided contact details clearly at the top of the resume. Don't forget to mention your email-id and phone numbers; preferably a mobile number – ensuring you never miss a call from the HR when he or she is looking for you.
5. **Multiple Resume:** It is not wrong to have multiple resume. It pays to customize your resume according to the company's requirement. For example, you might need to sell yourself for an "Embedded Programmer" job with your C knowledge and for an "Application Programmer" job you may need to emphasize on front end tools.

Note: Always keep copy of the resume with you, and whenever you are called for an interview, you must go through the resume submitted, and even can carry copy of the same with you in the interview. Your copy will help you to know what you have claimed in your resume.

Points to Remember

- Make sure you are familiar with what you write on your resume; and yes ensure that you are well prepared on all the facets of the topics you have touched upon. Your resume is the only source of information for the interviewer and all questions would invariably be directly linked to what you have mentioned.
- Be crisp and clear. In the project details section, it is recommended that you write about the responsibilities you handled in the project and what you have accomplished in this project rather than a lengthy essay about the nitty gritty of the project.
- Highlight technical accomplishments like certifications obtained, training attended, etc.
- Limit or avoid writing excessively about your personal details.
- You don't need to have declaration. Remember it is a resume and not a legal affidavit.

Sample Resume

A lot of material is available in literature about writing a good resume. The following sample resume can enlighten the reader as how a good resume should look. Take some time and try to put all your creativity into your resume.

Priti Sharma

F1-401, 4th Floor
Shourya Greens Apartments, Surya Enclave
Amritsar Byepass, Jalandhar-144009.

Modile: +91-98156-98156
Res: +91-181-2420004
E-mail: priti.sharma@gmail.com

Objective: To seek a challenging career in the field of design and development of software.

Professional Profile:

- Proficient in programming with C/C++ languages.
- Good team worker.
- Excellent communication skills.

Technical Skills:

Operating Systems	:	Windows XP/7, Linux
Programming Languages	:	C/C++/Core Java
Database	:	Oracle 10g, MySQL
Web Technologies	:	PHP, DHTML/XML, JSP

Experience:

Project #1:

Company: ABC India Pvt. Ltd. , Mohali.
Project Title: Design and Development of XXX (Academic Project)
Technology: Visual Basic, Oracle
Project: Give brief description of project and your role in the project.

Project #2:

Company: PVC India Pvt. Ltd., New delhi.
Project Title: Design and Development of YYY (Academic Project)
Technology: Linux, MySQL, PHP
Project: Give brief description of project and your role in the project.

Professional Qualification:

Bachelor of Technology in Computer Science & Engineering, Thapar University, Patiala, with First Class upto 7th Semester.

Semester 1	Semester 2	Semester 3	Semester 4
78 %	77 %	80 %	75 %

Semester 5	Semester 6	Semester 7	
80 %	75 %	82 %	

Academic Qualification:

+2 (CBSE Board), Apeejay School, Mahavir Marg, Jalndhar.
Aggregate Percentage : 85 %

Matriculation (CBSE Board), Apeejay School, Mahavir Marg, Jalndhar.
Aggregate Percentage : 80 %

Hobbies: Reading, sports, and interacting with people.

Soft Skills: Winning people, fast learner, and excellent communicator.

1.5.2 Preparing a Questionnaire

Prepare a comprehensive list of questions which are likely to come up in the interview. Once this list is ready, understand these questions and write down their answers in your own language. Grasp these answers because only then you will be able to answer these questions in a crispy manner when they are asked for during the interview.

1.5.3 Know the Potential Employer

Gathering background information about the potential employers is very crucial for successful interview preparation. This information will help you to know about the company profile, its financial health, technologies being used, HR policies, etc. During the interview, if you can demonstrate that you know a lot about the company, the interviewers will get a feeling that this candidate has a keen interest in our organization, and this factor can go in your favour.

1.5.4 Preparing for Handling the Interview

Most interviewers try to comfort the candidates during the initial session of the interview; hence they try to talk about personal details about which candidates are pretty comfortable talking about. This also opens up a channel of communication at a personal level. If you could impress the panel with well prepared/rehearsed crisp answers, your chances of success are assured better.

It is a scientifically proven fact that only about 10-20% of your communication depends on the words you speak and it contents. Over 80% of communication depends on hinges on other neuro-linguistic attributes like the tone of speech, fluency of expression and body language while delivering the contents. Hence, to get comfortable in such situations, organize/attend mock interviews among your peers and host group discussions to improve your communications skills.

1.5.4.1 Some of the Common Ice-Breakers

- Tell us some thing about you. OR Introduce yourself. OR Who are you?

  It is a million dollar question. The effective handling of this question is going to set the tone for rest of the interview – you can drive the interview or you are going to be driven by the interviewers.

  Give a good account of educational background, professional competencies and your passionate hobbies. Even before the actual technical interview begins you can strike a very positive chord with your interviewers by answering confidently and putting forth a concisely prepared brief. Keep it short and to the point. Never elaborate unless requested.

Here is a sample introduction:

I am Priti Sharma, daughter of Dr. L. R. Sharma and Mrs.Kusum Sharma. I passed my matriculation and Plus 2 examinations from Apeejay School, Jalandhar, with aggregate scores of 85% and 80%, respectively.

At present, I am pursuing my B. Tech. in CSE from Thapar University, Patiala, and my aggregate score stands at 82% upto 7th semester.

I am proficient in the subjects of Object-Oriented Programming using C++ and Data Structures. My other subjects of interest are Operating Systems and Software Engineering.

My core strengths are - I am a good communicator; I am a very positive person; I am very flexible and can adapt a new situation very quickly; I am a good team player; I am a fast learner; and above all a good human being.

My main weakness is that I am very emotional person.

My favorite hobbies include reading and interacting with people from different walks of life.

- What are your plans for pursuing higher education?

  Such questions are aimed at probing into your future retention value to the company. Companies would like to weed out any candidate who is looking at a stop-gap arrangement before they proceed on to their foreign universities.

- What has been the toughest challenge you have faced in your life so far? Describe your most successful moment in life.

  If you could give an interesting situation, which you faced in your life and how can you overcame adversity, it could help the panel in understanding your personality better. In all personal questions, be honest and truthful.

- What are your strengths and weaknesses?

  Do enumerate both of your personality preferably stressing on your strength with examples. Also show how you are working to improve your weaknesses.

- Why do you want to switch from your field (electronics, mechanical, etc.) to computer? Do you think you can cope with the pressure of learning a new domain?

Any non computer science student is bound to be asked this question. But giving a positive answer to this is very important. If you try to show that you are not interested in your own area of specialization and wish to move just because software looks rosy on the outside, you could be caught off-guard with follow-up questions like "After attending our training sessions if you suddenly realize that software is the place for you, what you will do? Try to depict your versatility and readiness to adapt to change in necessary.

- Give an example where you have taken initiative in your college. Have you ever organized a college tour/event? Give a brief account of your extracurricular life in college.

  Such questions are posed to test the leadership traits displayed by the candidates in their academic lives and would definitely go a long way in scoring extra points in your overall tally. This opportunity should be used to highlight any leadership initiative you have taken in leading a group towards a common goal.

1.5.4.2 Some of the Trap Questions

- Are you willing to travel to any city in India and even abroad?

  In software industry, the requirements for travel are very dynamic and every candidate is expected to give priority to project requirements, Unless you have serious traveling limitations, this issue is best postponed to when the actual travel need arises.

- Do you have any strong likes/dislikes with respect to technology? Do you mind working on maintenance projects?

  If you have a passion for a specific technology or domain, it wouldn't harm in letting them know about your interests and how your learning curve would be steeper if assigned to these assignments.

- Do you have any problem staying late in office or working on holidays as required?

  Late hour working and holidays skipping in an intrinsic part of the software professional's life. As freshers, all candidates are expected to understand and consent to this.

1.5.4.3 Other Questions to Test Your Emotional Maturity

- We see that your marks have not been consistent through your semesters, can you tell us why?
- Which do you think is more important – *individual brilliance, team effort* or *hard work*? Rank them in order of your importance.

- A lot of candidates with much better marks have also applied for this job, why should we consider you instead of them?

All projects, software or otherwise, require us to work in groups and be capable of dealing with the complexities arising from it. Coming out of academic life we often see that highly individualistic or uncommunicative people are not preferred everywhere. As always, virtues like hard work, perseverance, honesty, truthfulness and helpfulness are highly respected.

Some of the possible questions in which you could portray some of the high points of your academic career are:

- What do you consider to be your most significant achievement so far?
- In the software industry, what do you think is the most important characteristic of software professional?
- How do you see your career growth in this organization? Where do you see yourself three years from now?

You are the best person to answer these questions about yourself and the better you portray your self, the better it is for you. As these questions are about incidents in life you have experienced you should always have a couple of ready answers to these questions rather than thinking about them while on the hot seat!

The one question you must prepare for it . . .

Do you have any question for us?

This is usually the final question in the interview and should be seized by the candidate to show his interest in knowing the organization better and clarify any concerns he/she has.

This chapter would have given you a peek into the interview process and given an idea on the ground work you have to do before appearing in an campus interview.

The forthcoming chapters will give you an insight into the technical aspects of the interview, which are, of course, equally important.

Best of Luck!

❑ ❑ ❑

Chapter 2

Basic Computer Concepts

Question #1

Can computer be used to solve all sorts of problems?

Answer:

No. Only those kinds of problems can be solved by the computer which precisely can be expressed in the form of an algorithm.

Question #2

What is booting?

Answer:

Booting is a process in which your computer gets initialized. This process includes initializing all your hardware components in your computer and gets them to work together and to load your default operating system which will make your computer operational.

Question #3

What are various types of booting?

Answer:

The booting process is of two types:

- **Warm booting:** Where the Reset button or Ctrl+Alt+Del key combination is used to restart the system. Here the POST routine is skipped where many of the higher level functions on the motherboard, memory, keyboard, video adapter, floppy drive, etc. are checked.
- **Cold booting:** Where the power first applied and the system has to go through a number of stages like, Applying power, bootstrap, core tests, POST, finding the OS, loading the OS and establishing the environment.

Question #4

What is problem solving?

Answer:

You will not be able to solve a problem if you don't know the steps involved in solving that problem. The same principle applies to writing a program. A programmer cannot write instructions to be given to the computer unless the programmer knows how to solve the problem manually.

Therefore, it is very important that before attempting to write a program, the programmers must solve the problem manually. While solving a problem, the programmer will be able to learn about the various steps to be performed and the sequence in which these steps are to be performed.

Question #5

What is program planning and design?

Answer:

Planning is very important in every walk of life. Even for our routine kind of things, we have to plan. For example, we have to plan our monthly budget otherwise things can go astray and we may not enough money left in our pocket towards the end of the month. Planning should not be in the mind only, you must write it down, *i.e.*, you must document it.

Likewise, if you know the steps to be followed for solving a given problem but you have not documented them, you may forget to apply some of the steps or you may apply some of the steps in wrong sequence. Obviously, you will get a wrong answer. Similarly, while writing a program, if the programmer leaves out some of the instructions or writes the instructions in wrong sequence, the computer will give a wrong answer.

Therefore, in order to write an efficient and effective program, it is necessary that the programmer must write each and every instruction in the proper sequence. However, the sequence of instructions, *referred to as logic*, of a program can be very complex. Hence, in order to ensure that the program instructions are appropriate for the given problem and are in the correct sequence, programs must be planned before they are written.

Question #6

Name the various program design tools.

Answer:

The various program design tools are *algorithms, flowcharts, pseudocodes* and *decision tables*.

Question #7

What is an algorithm?

Answer:

An *algorithm* is defined as a finite sequence of instructions (steps) defining the solution of a particular problem, where each instruction is numbered and written using simple English language.

Question #8

What is a flowchart?

Answer:

A *flowchart* is a pictorial representation of an algorithm. A flowchart uses different shapes to denote different types of instructions. The actual instructions are written within the shapes using clear and concise statements. These shapes are connected by directed lines to indicate the sequence in which instructions are to be executed.

Question #9

What is a pseudocode?

Answer:

The word *pseudo* means imitation or false and the word *code* refers to the instruction written in a programming language. Pseudocode, therefore, is an imitation of actual computer instructions. These pseudo instructions are phrases written in English like statements. Instead of using symbols to describe the logic of the program, as in flowcharts, pseudocode uses a structure that resembles computer instructions.

Because, it emphasizes the design of the program, pseudocode is also called *Program Design Language* (PDL).

Question #10

What is a decision table?

Answer:

A *decision table* is another program development tool that is used as a supplement along with flowcharts. This tool is particularly useful in problems which involve complex decision making.

A decision table, shown in Figure 1.15, is a special table that is divided into four parts by a pair of horizontal and vertical lines.

		R_1	R_2	R_3	. . .	R_n	
	C_1						
	C_2						
Condition Stub	C_3				*Condition Row*		Condition Entries
	.						
	.						
	.						
	C_k						
	A_1						
	A_2						
Action Stub	A_3				*Action Row*		Action Entries
	.						
	.						
	.						
	A_m						

Figure 1.15: Decision table and its related terms

The part above the horizontal double lines pertains to the conditions being listed, *i.e.*, questions being asked, and the outcomes of these tests, *i.e.*, the answers to these questions. The part to the left of vertical double lines in the top portion, *i.e.*, above horizontal double lines, lists the conditions (C_is) is known as the *Condition Stub*. The part to the right of vertical double lines in the top portion lists the answers to these questions, namely Yes or No (which are usually abbreviated as Y and N), and is known as *Conditions Entries*. Each row in the top half of the table listing a question and its answer is known as *Condition Row*. The bottom half of the decision table, *i.e.*, the part below the pair of horizontal lines, lists the actions to be performed. The left part of the bottom portion is known as *Action Stub*, and in it the actions ($A_i s$) to be carried out are listed. The right part of the bottom portion has crosses 'X' and dashes '-' to be carried out are listed. A cross indicates that the action in that row is to be performed and a dash indicates that the action is not to be performed. These are called *Action Entries*. Each row in the lower portion is called an *Action Row*. The columns to the right of the vertical pair of double lines are called *Rules* ($R_i s$). A rule is interpreted by using the conditions listed in the condition stub and the answers listed in the condition entries. The corresponding actions are obtained from the action stub and action entries.

Question #11

What is Open-Source Software?

Answer:

Open-Source Software (OSS) is computer software that is available in source code form. The source code and certain other rights normally reserved for copyright holders are provided under a free software license that permits users to study, change, improve and at times also to distribute the software.

Question #12

Name some of the popular open-source software.

Answer:

Most popular open-source software includes the following:

- **Linux:** an operating system and kernel originating as a UNIX system and existing in many versions. For more information visit *http://www.linux.org*.
- **MySQL:** is an open source RDBMS. It is very fast reliable and flexible. For more information visit *http://www.mysql.com.*
- **GNOME:** a desktop development environment providing tools for developing desktop applications (as well as its own basic desktop applications) and available for Linux and other UNIX systems. For more information visit *http://www.gnome.org.*
- **Apache:** a web server program (for supplying pages in response to requests) used in most web server computers and available for Windows as well as Linux and other UNIX systems. For more information visit *http://www.apache.org/.*

- **Firefox:** a web client program (for viewing and hearing web pages) available for Windows and Mac as well as Linux and other UNIX systems. For more information visit *http://www.mozilla.org/firefox.*
- **Postfix:** an email server program (for sending and receiving email) supporting SMTP and available for Linux and other UNIX systems. For more information visit *http://www.postfix.org.*
- **OpenOffice:** an office application set (for word processing, spreadsheet manipulation, picture drawing and data base access) compatible with all other major office application sets such as Office and is available for Windows, Mac, Linux and UNIX operating systems. For more information visit *http://www.openoffice.org.*

Question #13

What is FOSS?

Answer:

FOSS stands for Free and Open-Source Software. It is the kind of software that is both free and open source. It is liberally licensed to grant users the right to use, copy, study, change, and improve its design through the availability of its source code.

Question #14

What is freeware?

Answer:

Freeware is software that you can download off the Internet and use for free. However freeware may not always provide much help in terms of support if the software goes wrong, so there is always a certain amount of risk when using freeware.

While freeware will be free for use, for home users, and without restrictions, this may not be the case for commercial use. The software license will indicate if academic and commercial use will be prohibited or not.

Question #15

Differentiate computer organization and computer architecture.

Answer:

Following table sums up the differences computer organization & computer architecture:

Computer Organization	Computer Architecture
It refers to operational units and their interconnections that realize the architectural specifications.	It refers to those attributes of a system that are visible to a programmer. In other words, those attributes that have a direct impact on the logical execution of the program.
Examples of organizational attributes include those hardware details that are transparent to programmer such as control signals, interfaces between processor and peripherals, the technology used for memory, etc.	Examples of architectural attributes include the instruction set, the number of bits used to represent various data types, I/O mechanisms, addressing modes, etc.

Computer architecture comes before computer organization. It is like building the design and architecture of the house which takes maximum time and then organization is building the house by bricks or by latest technology keeping the basic layout and architecture of house in mind.

Question #16

Differentiate between CISC and RISC.

Answer:

Following table sums up the differences between CISC and RISC:

CISC	RISC
1. CISC stands for Complex Instruction Set Computer.	1. RISC stands for Reduced Instruction Set Computers.
2. It has a bigger instruction set with many addressing modes.	2. It has a smaller instruction set with few addressing modes
3. It has to use a separate micro-programming unit with a control memory to implement complex instructions.	3. It has a hard-wired programmed-unit without a control memory, and separate hardware to implement each and every instruction.
4. An easy compiler design	4. A complex compiler design.
5. The calculations are slower and precise	5. The calculations are faster and precise
6. Decoding of instruction is complex	6. Decoding of instruction is simple.
7. The Execution time is very high.	7. It takes a very less execution time.
8. It frequently needs the external memory access to make calculations.	8. Since it uses a hardwired model, its not often, to take the external memory access for calculations.
9. Pipelining does not function correctly here because of complexity in instructions.	9. Pipelining is not a major problem and this option speeds up the processors.
10. These processors often stall because of pipelining problem.	10. Since the instructions are not complex, stalling is mostly reduced.
11. Code Expansion is not a problem in CISC processors.	11. Code expansion can be a problem in some cases in RISC processors.
12. Disc space is wasted.	12. Disc space is saved.
13. Used in low end applications such us security systems, home automation, etc.	13. Used in high end applications such us video processing, telecommunications, image processing, etc.

Question #17

What is the little endian and big endian?

Answer:

Endianness is the attribute of a processor that determines whether the operands are stored from lower memory towards higher memory or from higher memory towards lower memory.

Little endian means that the lower-order byte of the number is stored in memory at the lower address and the higher-order byte is stored at the higher address (the little end comes first.)

For example, a 4 byte *long int*

```
Byte3 Byte2 Byte1 Byte0
```

will be arranged in memory as follows:

```
Base Address+0    Byte0
Base Address+1    Byte1
Base Address+2    Byte2
Base Address+3    Byte3
```

Intel processors (those used in PC's) use Little Endian byte order.

Big Endian means that the high-order byte of the number is stored in memory at the lower address, and the low-order byte at the higher address. (the big end comes first.)

Our *long int*, would then be stored as:

```
Base Address+0    Byte3
Base Address+1    Byte2
Base Address+2    Byte1
Base Address+3    Byte0
```

Motorola processors (those used in Mac's) use Big Endian byte order.

Question #18

What is cache memory?

Answer:

Cache memory is an extremely fast, small memory between CPU and main memory, whose access time is closer to the processing speed of the CPU. It acts as a high speed buffer between CPU and main memory, and is used to temporarily store very active data and instructions during processing.

Question #19

What is L1 and L2 cache memory?

Answer:

L1 cache is some kind of memory which is built into the same CPU and it is the place where the CPU first try to access. The L2 cache is another memory but instead of feeding the CPU, this one feeds the L1 cache and this way L2 cache can be under stood as a cache of the L1 cache.

Question #20

What is virtual memory?

Answer:

It is a memory management scheme that allows the execution of processes which might not be completed loaded in the main memory. The three basic concept use for the realization of virtual memory are *online secondary storage*, *swapping* and *demand paging*.

Question #21

What is memory hierarchy?

Answer:

Memory hierarchy is a ranking of computer memory devices, with devices having the fastest access time at the top of the hierarchy, and devices with slower access times but larger capacity and lower cost at lower levels.

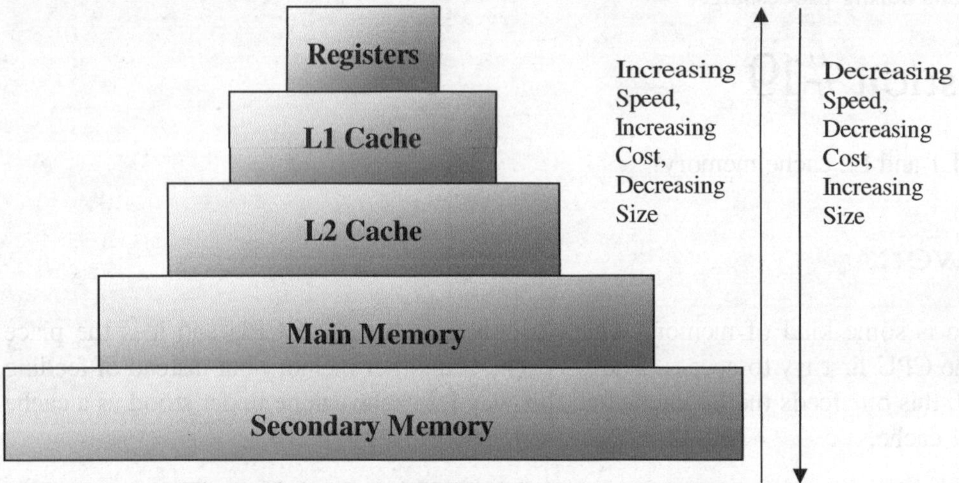

Figure 2.1: Memory Hierarchy

Question #22

What is a programming paradigm?

Answer:

A programming paradigm is a fundamental style of computer programming which usually differs in the concepts and abstractions used to represent the elements of a program (such as objects, functions, variables, constraints...) and the steps that compose a computation (assignation, evaluation, continuations, data flows...).

Question #23

What is the difference between procedural and non-procedural languages?

Answer:

Procedural Languages	Non-Procedural Languages
Even for a simple task, we have to develop a procedure (a set of instructions) to complete a task. Majority of the high-level languages fall into this category.	You don't have to write a procedure for simple and routine type tasks. Structured Query Language (SQL) is an example of such a language. It allows inserting, deleting and retrieving data from the database without writing the procedure.

Question #24

What is a compiler?

Answer:

A compiler is a program that takes source code as its input, check the entire program instruction-by-instruction for its grammatical accuracy, and if the source code is grammatical accurate, then it translates the program again instruction-by-instruction to machine language and writes to the disk file

Question #25

What is an interpreter?

Answer:

An Interpreter is a program that takes source code as its input, translates one line of the source code at a time and executes the translated instruction.

Although interpreters run programs more slowly than programs compiled into object code, they are helpful tool for learning and debugging. As the program executes line by line the programmer can see exactly what each line does.

Note that in order to execute (run) a program using interpreter, first we need to run the interpreter, then only we can instruct the interpreter the run the user program. Therefore, every time to run the user program you need to run the interpreter as well.

Question #26

Compare and contrast between a compiler and an interpreter.

Answer:

The following table sums up the comparison between a Compiler and an interpreter

Compiler	Interpreter
It takes entire program as unit of translation and does not execute the program.	It translates one instruction at a time and executes it.
After translation, it writes the object code onto a disk file.	It translates instruction by instruction and does not create a permanent object code.
It does not execute the program after translation.	It executes every instruction after translation and continues doing so till all the instructions are finished.
After translation, neither the source code nor the compiler is required for executing the program.	Both, interpreter as well the source code are required for execution of the program. In fact, first interpreter program is executed, and then it is instructed to execute the program under consideration.
Program execution is very fast since the object code is directly executed.	Program execution is slow since each instruction is translated first and then executed.
Compilers play almost no role in debugging, since after compilation, the compiler is not in picture and have no role during program execution.	Debugging is very easy since each instruction is executed one-by-one, programmer and/or user can see what each instruction does.
To execute the program on a different computer, you need to compile the program on that computer. It will be essential sometimes since it may have different machine language	However, if you have an interpreter on another machine, the program can be executed as such since translation takes place during execution, and will take place automatically.
Well suited for application where high performance is the need.	Well suited for the beginners who are just learning the particular high-level language.

Question #27

What is an editor?

Answer:

Editor is a program that allows creating and editing of files. Further, there are editors that allow working with text files only, and are called *text editors*. Examples of popular text editors are *notepad* and *edit* of *Windows* operating system, *vi* of *Unix* and *Linux* operating systems.

Question #28

What is a linker?

Answer:

Linker is a program that combines the object of the program with the object codes of the library and user-defined functions, in the desired manner, and writes the same in a separate program file with extension, usually EXE under Windows. This file produced by the linker is known as *executable file* or simply as *run file*, and is the file that is used to execute the program.

Question #29

What is a loader?

Answer:

Loader is a program that is responsible for transferring the executable file from the secondary storage to memory. On execution, the loader, with the assistance of the operating system, first finds the free memory of the requisite amount and then transfers the executable file into that part of memory, takes appropriates steps such as address translation, and then initiates its execution. From that point onwards, the role of the loader is over, and the control is taken over by the program. The instruction of the program are executed to perform the desired task, but under the overall supervision of the operating system. As soon as the program finishes its execution, it is removed from the memory.

Question #30

What is a debugger?

Answer:

All sort of errors that are encountered during program development (syntax errors, logical error and runtime/execution errors) are known as bugs, and the process of identifying those errors and fixing (correcting) them is known as *debugging*. The logical errors are most difficult to track. To catch logical errors, we need to observe the pattern in which the instructions of the program are executed and the intermediate and final results are produced.

Debugger is a program that, in general, allows user to monitor the trace the execution of executable version of program.

Question #31

What is a programming environment?

Answer:

Programming environment is an environment in which programs are created and tested, and it has less influence on the design of the language that the operating environment on which the programs are expected to be run.

A programming environment consists of support tools and a command language (set of commands) to invoke them. Each support tool is another program that may be used by the programmer as an aid during one or more stages of creation of a program.

Typical tools in a programming environment include *editors, language translators, linkers, loaders, test data generators*, etc.

Question #32

What is a runtime environment (RTE)?

Answer:

It is the environment provided the run-time system which is a software component designed to support the execution of computer programs written in some computer language.

The run-time system contains implementations of basic low-level commands and may also implement higher-level commands and may support type checking, debugging, and even code generation and optimization.

Some services of the run-time system are accessible to the programmer through an application programming interface (API), but other services (such as task scheduling and resource management) may be inaccessible.

Question #33

What is a structured programming?

Answer:

It is a programming technique that assumes the disciplined use of a few coding structures (sequence, selection, and iteration) and the use of top-down concepts to decompose main functions into lower-level components for modular programming.

The main aim of this technique is to improve the programming process through better organization and with better programming notations to facilitate correct and clear description of data and control structures.

Question #34

What is a modular programming?

Answer:

It is a programming technique that produces relatively small, easily understandable modules. A complex or large program is broken into number of logically self-contained modules. These modules may be written and tested separately by number of programmers. Finally, the modules are put together to form a complete program.

Question #35

What is a module?

Answer:

It is a subprogram carrying out a particular task and can be called by another module, known as the calling module. A module needs to be placed only once in memory and can be called by the main module or other modules as many times as the programmer wants. Modules are also known by various names such as *function*, *subroutine* or *procedure*.

Question #36

What is a structured programming language? Give few examples of structured programming language.

Answer:

A language is said to be a structured language if it meets the requirements of structured programming. Examples include Pascal, C, etc.

Question #37

What is a *source code, object code* and *executable code*?

Answer:

Source code is a program written in a high-level level language, such as C.

Object code is a translated version of source code in machine language.

Executable code is a final version of program, in machine language, that is executed on user's command.

Question #38

What is a translation unit?

Answer:

A translation unit is a set of files seen by the compiler. It includes the source code under consideration and files that are included such as header files in C/C++ languages, and other disk files contains C code.

Question #39

What is an error? What are different types of errors?

Answer:

An error is the encoding of human misunderstanding of some aspect of programming language or problem under consideration.

The types of errors are *syntax error*, *logical error*, and *runtime error*.

Syntax errors result from the violation of the grammar (syntax) of C language. In the presence of syntax errors, the program will not compile.

Logical errors result from the wrong logic that in turn result from the poor understanding of the problem under consideration. Even in the presence of logical errors, the program will run but the results will be incorrect. These errors are most difficult to locate particularly if the problem is large and complex.

Runtime errors result either from non-availability of the resource required such an attempt to open/read from a non-existing data file or memory allocation failure, etc.; or an attempt to perform an illegal operation such as division by zero, taking square root or logarithm of a negative number, etc. In the presence of these errors, the program will terminate prematurely, *i.e.*, before finishing its intended task. Premature termination is also known as abnormal terminal.

Errors are also known as *bugs*.

Question #40

What is debugging?

Answer:

It is the process of locating and correcting the bugs.

Question #41

What is bebugging?

Answer:

It is the process of injecting known bugs in a program in order to train the students in debugging.

Question #42

The output produced by a compiler is an object code, *i.e.*, machine code, but not in a form that can be executed. Why?

Answer:

Recall that a program can contain calls to library function as well as user-defined functions that are in other disk files and are not included using *file inclusion* preprocessor directive (#include).

The compiler doesn't have access to the definitions of these functions, and hence can't bind the function calls to function definitions. Hence, function calls are left unresolved. In addition, some more information is required by the operating system to run the program.

Question #43

What happens during linking?

Answer:

The next step after compilation is linking, *i.e.*, to resolve the unresolved references to functions. This task is accomplished by another program known as *linker*. The linker takes object code(s) as its inputs and searches for unresolved references. For every unresolved reference, it searches libraries for their definitions and adds them to the end of final code being generated and fills its address at point of call. If search of any function is unsuccessful, the linker will generate a message like unresolved references and the also gives the name of the function called.

It also adds more information in the header of the executable file, for example Program Segment Prefix (PSP) as was with MS DOS operating system, plus address relocation information, etc.

The output of a linker is a machine language program that is in executable form better known as executable code or run file.

Question #44

What is relocation? Why is it necessary?

Answer:

Relocation means modifying the existing addresses of program code and data.

To understand why, let us dig deeper:

Your program may consist of many separate compilation units and hence separate object codes for each translation unit. Compiler will assign addresses to each of the translation unit from the same base address. Hence, there will be a clash of address as such. Therefore, during linking, when the linker combines these object codes and library function, it combines these object codes end-to-end, and each object codes gets starting address after that address where it predecessor has finished, and accordingly all other relative address are modified.

Also when you give a command to run the program, the operating system first allocates a block of memory from free memory in RAM, and then invokes the *loader*. Loader is a program, which is usually part of the operating system, which reads your program from the disk and loads into main memory allocated by the operating system. Here also it is important to mention that address of the allocated block is different from the starting address of the executable code, the loader also modifies the relative address of the executable address so that it can run successfully from its new address space.

Question #45

What are the different types of addresses in a program?

Answer:

There are two types of addresses: *absolute addresses* and *relative addresses*.

Absolute addresses are those addresses that are fixed and never changes such as addresses of I/O and other ports, etc.

On the other hand, relative addresses are those addresses that depend on the starting address of the object code such as addresses of instructions and operands (variables and constants declared and defined in a function). Whenever, the starting address of the object code is changed, these addresses also need to be changed.

Question #46

What happens when the user gives a command to run a program?

Answer:

The operating system first allocates the requisite amount of memory to the program, then, through loader, loads the program in the allocated memory, and then passes on the control to the program. The program runs the supervision of the operating system. When the program finishes its execution or some runtime errors occur, the operating system removes the program from the memory.

Question #47

Is there any type of programs that remains in memory after finishing their execution, and are removed only explicitly?

Answer:

Yes, these programs are known as Terminate and Stay Resident (TSR) programs. Examples of such programs are screen savers, virus guards, etc. These programs are usually event driven programs, *i.e.*, they start/stop executing whenever the appropriate event occurs.

For example, all screen savers provide the features where you can set the waiting time (in minutes). Whenever there is no keyboard or mouse activity, the screen saver starts executing and as soon as you press any key or move/click the mouse, the screen saver terminates.

Question #48

What is hardware?

Answer:

Hardware refers to the parts of a computer that you can see and touch, including the case and everything inside it.

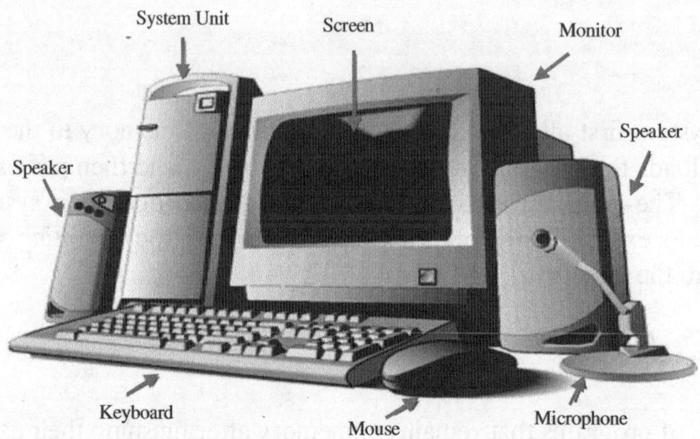

Figure 1.4: Typical home PC

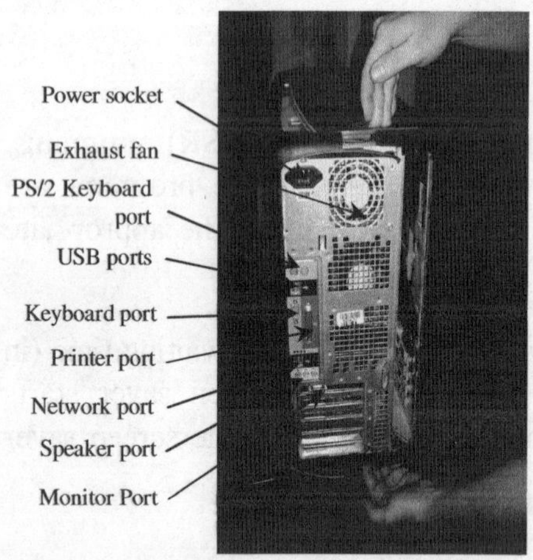

(*a*) Back panel of system unit

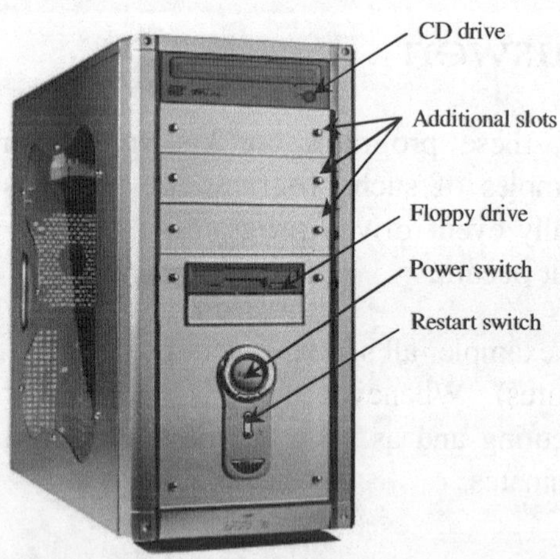

(*b*) Front panel of system unit

Figure 1.5: Outside view of the system unit

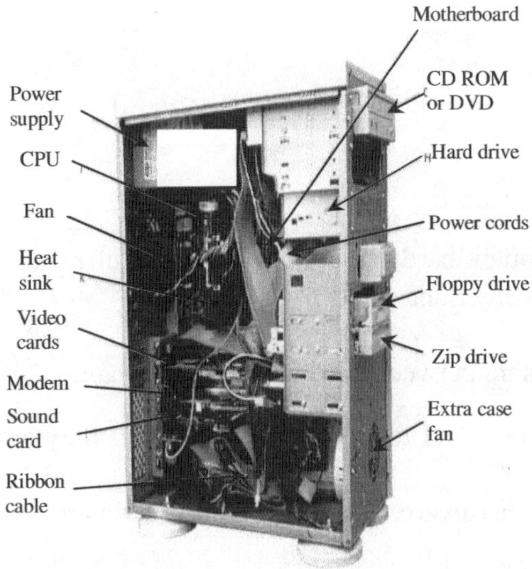

Figure 1.6: Inside view of the system

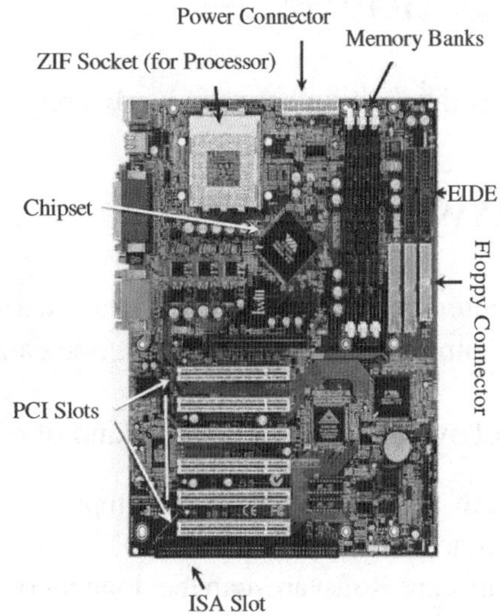

Figure 1.7: Typical Motherboard

Question #49

What is software?

Answer:

A said earlier, a computer cannot do anything without proper instructions from the user. It needs to be instructed to do a specific job. This set of instructions for a specific job is called *computer program.* The computer program (set of instructions) is written using desired programming language.

Software, basically, a generic name for any kind of computer program.

Question #50

What is the relation between hardware and software?

Answer:

Computer software works together with computer hardware to produce useful results. Both compliment each other, *i.e.*, one cannot do any thing on its own.

The following points signify the kind of relationship between hardware and software:

- Both are necessary for a computer to function and to do useful work, *i.e.*, they are complementary.
- Different software can be loaded on same hardware. This way same hardware can perform variety of tasks.
- Except for upgrades (like increasing the RAM, increasing hard disk capacity, adding speakers, modem, etc.), hardware is normally a one time cost, whereas software involves variable cost. For example, software upgrades or buying and loading a new software for performing different kind of task.
- In the early computing days, hardware was expensive than software and the effort was to reduce the cost. With the advances in semiconductors and microelectronics, purchasing a computer is now within the reach of a common man.
- In present days, the cost of software (as computers are beings used to perform much complex and difficult tasks) is much more than the hardware.

Question #51

What are the major categories of software?

Answer:

The major categories of the software *system software*, *application software*, *firmware*, *utility software* and *packages*.

Question #52

What is system software?

Answer:

System software constitutes all that set of programs that are required either to control the operations of or to provide an environment for developing application as well as other type of software.

In general, system software performs one or more of the following functions:

- Monitors the efficient use hardware resources such as CPU, memory, peripherals, etc.
- Communicates with and controls the operations of peripherals such as printers, disks, modems, etc.
- Supports the development of application and other type of software.
- Supports the execution of application and other type of software.

The prominent programs that come under the umbrella of system software are *operating systems*, *editors*, *compilers*, *interpreters*, *linkers*, *loaders*, *debuggers*, etc. These programs are written by specialist programmers, who have sound knowledge of hardware of the computer, and are called *system programmers*.

Question #53

What is an operating system?

Answer:

The most important program on any computer is the *Operating System* or simply OS. The OS is a large program made up of many smaller programs. It acts as resource manager of the computer system and provides an interface between the users and the hardware. The resources of a computer system include processor, memories and I/O devices. As a manager it coordinates the activities of various resources so as to provide the users with the required information.

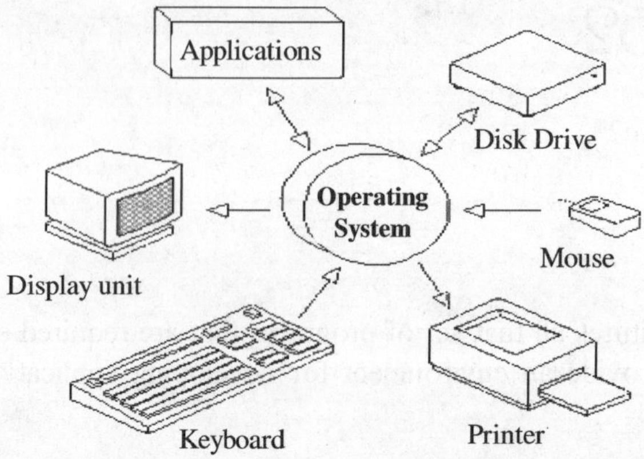

Figure 1.1: Operating system communicating with various devices and applications

Examples of popular operator systems include *Microsoft Windows* family, *Linux* & *Unix*.

Question #54

What are the main functions of an operating system?

Answer:

The main function performed by operating system include *process management*, *memory management*, *file management*, *security* and *command interpretation*.

Question #55

What is application software?

Answer:

Application software constitutes all that set of programs that are developed by the developers for their own use or to be used by their clients. Applications software is developed using system software.

The application software can be developed using appropriate programming language. There are large numbers of programming languages and each programming language is developed targeting a specific domain or set of specific domains.

Application software for most of the current projects is either being developed using *Java technologies* or *.NET technologies.*

Question #56

What is firmware?

Answer:

Firmware is a combination of both hardware and software. Special tools are used for developing these programs. Here, the software is developed for specific applications and then it is written (embedded) into ROM. These programs are, usually, provided by the computer manufacturing firm, that is why, they are known as *firmware.*

Examples of firmware are *Power On Self Test* (POST) program, *bootstrap loader* and *micro-programmed control unit* of a computer system.

Question #57

What is utility software?

Answer:

Utility software refers to kind of programs that are developed to perform certain routine type tasks such as taking regular *backups*, *recovering* data when the system is put on track after a system crash, etc.

Question #58

What is a package?

Answer:

Package refers to a software or bundled suite of software that is developed by an individual or an enterprise. These packages are used to solve problems in specific domains or they provide an environment for solving problems as well as for developing software to solve problems in specified domains.

Examples of packages are *MS Office Suite* from Microsoft, *MS Visual Studio* also from Microsoft, *Open Office* – an open source software, etc.

Question #59

What is software development life cycle?

Answer:

Software development life cycle (SDLC) is a systematic way of developing quality software. It provides an organized plan for breaking down the task of software development into manageable chunks, each of which must be successfully completed before moving on to the next phase.

The software development process is divided into following phases:

- Problem definition
- Requirement analysis
- System design
- Implementation (Coding)
- Testing
- Deployment
- Maintenance

Question #60

List the advantages of high-level languages (HLL)?

Answer:

Significant advantages of high-level languages include:

1. They are easy to learn and use because they are similar to the languages used by us in our day to day life.
2. The effort required to write instructions in HLLs is very less as compared to low-level languages.
3. They are machine independent, and thus programs written using HLLs can be used on any computer.
4. Program written in HLLs can be easily understood, and hence modification can be done with quite ease.

Question #61

In which of the language(s), one instruction in non-machine language gets translated to one machine language instruction?

Answer:

Assembly language only. Each instruction in assembly language gets translated to one machine language instruction whereas in all high-level languages, a single instruction (statement) may get translated into many machine language instructions.

Question #62

What is verification and validation?

Answer:

During the entire software development life cycle, following activities are undertaken:

- *Verification:* This activity is undertaken to ensure that at each phase, selected industry standards and procedures are applied.
- *Validation:* This activity is undertaken to ensure that each phase meets the stated requirements. If it does not, we may have to go to previous phase which may ultimately trace to the problem definition.

Question #63

What is pipeline processing?

Answer:

A technique that allows a computer processing operation to be broken down into several steps so that the individual step output can be handled by the computer in parallel.

Question #64

What is Direct Memory Access (DMA)?

Answer:

A type of I/O technique in which data can be transferred between the main memory and external devices without the main processor's involvement.

Question #65

What is cloud computing?

Answer:

Cloud computing is a comprehensive solution that delivers IT as a service. It is an Internet-based computing solution where shared resources are provided like electricity distributed on the electrical grid. Computers in the cloud are configured to work together and the various applications use the collective computing power as if they are running on a single system.

Question #66

What is grid computing?

Answer:

Grid computing is the act of sharing tasks over multiple computers. Tasks can range from data storage to complex calculations and can be spread over large geographical distances. Computers within a grid are used, normally, when they are not in use.

The various computers on the grid join together to create a virtual supercomputer. These computers can work on the same problems, traditionally reserved for supercomputers, and yet this network of computers is more powerful than the super computers built in the seventies and eighties. Modern supercomputers are built on the principles of grid computing, incorporating many smaller computers into a larger whole.

Question #67

What is green computing?

Answer:

Green computing, green IT or ICT Sustainability, refers to environmentally sustainable computing or IT. It is defined as the study and practice of designing, manufacturing, using, and disposing of computers, servers, and associated subsystems — such as monitors, printers, storage devices, and networking and communications systems — efficiently and effectively with minimal or no impact on the environment.

The goals of green computing are similar to green chemistry; reduce the use of hazardous materials, maximize energy efficiency during the product's lifetime, and promote the recyclability or biodegradability of defunct products and factory waste.

Research continues into key areas such as making the use of computers as energy-efficient as possible, and designing algorithms and systems for efficiency-related computer technologies.

Question #68

What is pervasive/ubiquitous computing?

Answer:

Pervasive computing (ubiquitous computing) is the growing trend towards embedding microprocessors in everyday objects so they can communicate information. The words pervasive and ubiquitous mean *existing everywhere*. Pervasive computing devices are completely connected and constantly available.

Pervasive computing relies on the convergence of wireless technologies, advanced electronics and the Internet. The goal of researchers working in pervasive computing is to create smart products that communicate unobtrusively. The products are connected to the Internet and the data they generate is easily available.

An example of a practical application of pervasive computing is the replacement of old electric meters with smart meters. In the past, electric meters had to be manually read by a company representative. Smart meters report usage in real-time over the Internet. They will also notify the power company when there is an outage, reset thermostats according to the homeowner's directives, send messages to display units in the home and regulate the water heater.

Question #69

What is transparent computing?

Answer:

Transparent computing is a characteristic of pervasive computing, the possible future state in which we will be surrounded by computers everywhere in the environment that respond to our needs without our conscious use.

In this context, transparent means invisible. A long sought goal of computer science, transparent computing would involve systems so subtle and responsive that they could, for example, solve various user problems without any knowledge on the part of the user of what was taking place.

Question #70

What are wearable computers?

Answer:

Wearable computers are miniature electronic devices that are worn by the bearer under, with or on top of clothing. This class of wearable technology has been developed for general or special purpose information technologies and media development. Wearable computers are especially useful for applications that require more complex computational support than just hardware coded logics.

One of the main features of a wearable computer is consistency. There is a constant interaction between the computer and user, *i.e.*, there is no need to turn the device on or off. Another feature is the ability to multi-task. It is not necessary to stop what you are doing to use the device; it is augmented into all other actions. These devices can be incorporated by the user to act like a prosthetic. It can therefore be an extension of the user's mind and/or body.

Question #71

What is Near Field Communication (NFC)?

Answer:

Near Field Communication (NFC) is a set of standards for smart phones and similar devices to establish radio communication with each other by touching them together or bringing them into close proximity, usually no more than a few centimeters. Present and anticipated applications include contact less transactions, data exchange, and simplified setup of more complex communications such as Wi-Fi.

Question #72

What is DNA computing?

Answer:

DNA computing is a form of computing which uses DNA and molecular biology, instead of the traditional silicon-based computer technologies.

This field was initially developed by Leonard Adleman of the University of Southern California. In 1994, Adleman demonstrated a proof-of-concept use of DNA as form of computation which was used to solve the seven-point Hamiltonian path problem. Since the initial Adleman experiments, advances have been made, and various Turing machines have been proven to be constructable.

Question #73

What is quantum computing?

Answer:

Quantum computing is the area of study focused on developing computer technology based on the principles of quantum theory, which explains the nature and behavior of energy and matter on the quantum (atomic and subatomic) level.

Development of a quantum computer, if practical, would mark a leap forward in computing capability far greater than that from the abacus to a modern day supercomputer, with performance gains in the billion-fold realm and beyond. The quantum computer, following the laws of quantum physics, would gain enormous processing power through the ability to be in multiple states, and to perform tasks using all possible permutations simultaneously.

Current centers of research in quantum computing include MIT, IBM, Oxford University, and the Los Alamos National Laboratory

Question #74

Tell us, in brief, about NASSCOM.

Answer:

NASSCOM (National Association of Software and Services COMpanies) is a trade association of Indian Information Technology (IT) and Business Process Outsourcing (BPO) industry. It was established in the year 1988.

NASSCOM is a non-profit organization focused on promoting sustainable growth for the industry and to harness IT and communications technologies for inclusive and balanced growth.

Question #75

Tell us, in brief, about CSI.

Answer:

CSI (Computer Society of India), formed in 1965, has been instrumental in guiding the Indian IT industry down the right path since its formative years.

The mission of the CSI is to facilitate research, knowledge sharing, learning and career enhancement for all categories of IT professionals, while simultaneously inspiring and nurturing new entrants into the industry and helping them to integrate into the IT community. The CSI is also working closely with other industry associations, government bodies and academia to ensure that the benefits of IT advancement ultimately percolate down to every single citizen of India.

Question #76

Tell us, in brief, about ISTE.

Answer:

ISTE (Indian Society for Technical Education) is a national, professional, non-profit making Society registered under the Societies Registration Act of 1860. First started in 1941 as the Association of Principals of Technical Institutions (APTI), it was converted into "Indian Society for Technical Education" in 1968 with a view to enlarge its activities to advance the cause of technological education.

The major objective of the ISTE is to assist and contribute in the production and development of top quality professional engineers and technicians needed by the industries and other organizations. Being the only national organization of educators in the field of Engineering and Technology, ISTE effectively contributes in various missions of the Union Government.

Question #77

Tell us, in brief, about IETE.

Answer:

IETE (Institution of Electronics and Telecommunication Engineers), founded in 1953, is India's leading recognized professional society devoted to the advancement of Science and Technology of Electronics, Telecommunication & IT.

It provides leadership in Scientific and Technical areas of direct importance to the national development and economy. Government of India has recognized IETE as a Scientific and Industrial Research Organization (SIRO) and also notified as an educational Institution of national eminence.

The objectives of IETE focus on advancing electro-technology. The IETE conducts and sponsors technical meetings, conferences, symposia, and exhibitions all over India, publishes technical journals and provides continuing education as well as career advancement opportunities to its members.

Question #78

Tell us, in brief, about IE.

Answer:

IE (Institution of Engineers) is an international institution dedicated to educating business leaders through programs based on our core values of global focus, entrepreneurial spirit and a humanistic approach.

At IE, 500-strong, international faculty teaches a student body composed of more than 90 nationalities on its Undergraduate (IE University), Master, and Doctorate degrees, and Executive Education programs. IE alumni, now numbering over 37,000 (approx), hold management positions in some 100 countries worldwide.

IE champion high-quality research coupled with multidisciplinary, integrative education programs. Designed to address market demands, its innovative learning processes comprise a blend of online and onsite formats, making IE a pioneer in international education.

Question #79

Tell us, in brief, about IEEE.

Answer:

The Institute of Electrical and Electronics Engineers (IEEE, read I-Triple-E) is a non-profit professional association headquartered in New York City that is dedicated to advancing technological innovation and excellence.

It has more than 400,000 members in more than 160 countries, about 55% of whom reside in the United States.

Question #80

Tell us, in brief, about ACM.

Answer:

The Association for Computing Machinery (ACM) is a learned society for computing. It was founded in 1947 and is the world's largest and most prestigious scientific and educational computing society. It has more than 92,000 members. Its headquarters are in New York City.

ACM and the IEEE Computer Society are the primary umbrella organizations for academic and scholarly interests in computing.

Unlike the IEEE, however, the ACM is solely dedicated to computing.

❑ ❑ ❑

Chapter 3

The C Language

Question #1

Whether C language is *low-level*, *high-level*, or *middle-level* language?

Answer

The C language is a *middle-level* language. It is called a *middle- level* language because it has features of *high-level* language as well as *low-level* language.

Question #2

List the key characteristics of C language.

Answer

The C language was and will remain as one of the popular programming languages. Some of the key characteristics that add to its popularity are:

- It is a general purpose programming language, and therefore, can be used to solve vide variety of problems.
- It is supports structuring programming, and therefore, programs developed in it can easily be understood.

- It is free form, *i.e.*, no rigid format for writing programs. Any instruction can start from anywhere and end anywhere. In addition, a single instruction can span (can be written in) many lines.
- It is case sensitive. It distinguishes between lowercase (small) and uppercase (capital) alphabets.
- It was the first language to provide rich set of operators.
- It allows you, through pointers, to access any storage location and the devices connected to your computer through your program.
- It allows you to manipulate internal processor registers, and thus it is very useful for low-level programming.
- It is portable, that means any program written in it can be used on any computer without or with little modification(s).
- It allows you to develop your own library of functions that can be linked to your any program like standard library functions.

Question #3

List the main application areas of C language.

Answer

The strengths of C language make it a natural choice for following application areas:

- Systems programming that include writing software for language translators, device drivers, editors, linkers, loaders, etc.
- Network software to implement different communication protocols.
- Graphics programming that include writing software for graphical user interfaces (GUIs), scientific visualization, and presentation graphics, etc.
- Embedded systems where C routines are interfaced high speed assembly language routines and the resulting code is stored in ROM chip which is a part of the embedded system.

Question #4

Explain the general structure of a C program.

Answer

The usual order of statements written in a C program is as follows:

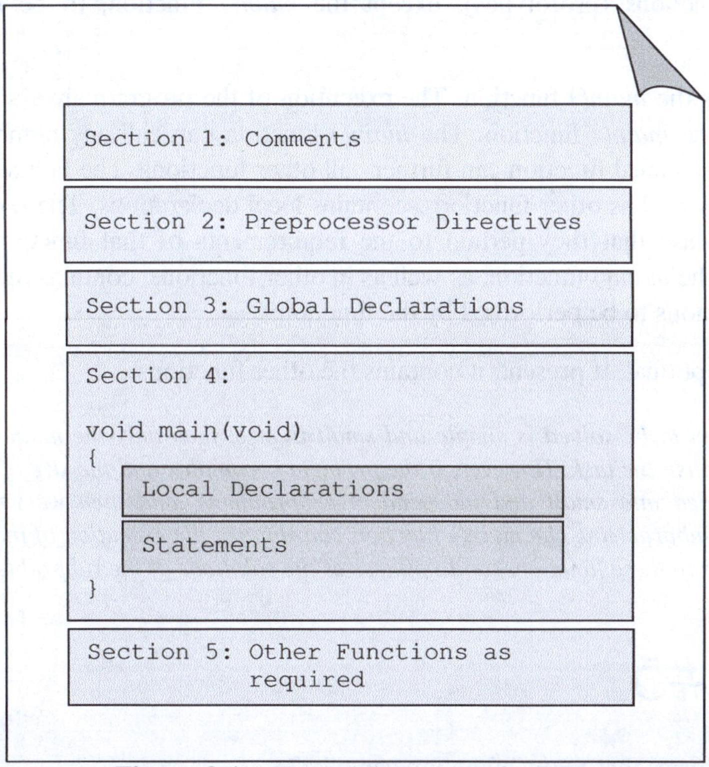

Figure 3.1: General Structure of a C Program

Section 1 is optional. If present it contains the description about the program. This description usually contains the information about the task being accomplished by the program. In addition, it can also contain the name of the author (programmer), the date on which it was written, the date on which it was last modified, etc.

Section 2 contains the preprocessor directives. The frequently used preprocessor directives are *include* and *define*. These directives tell the preprocessor how to prepare the program for compilation. The *include* directive tells which header files are to be included in the program and the *define* directive is usually used to associate an identifier with a literal (constant) that is to be used at many places in the program.

Section 3 is optional. If present, it contains the global declarations. These declarations usually include the declaration of the data items (variables) which are to be shared between many functions in the program. In addition, these declarations can also include the decorations of functions (prototypes), except the *main()* function, to be used in the program.

Section 4 contains the *main()* function. The execution of the program always begins with the execution of the *main()* function. The *main()* function can call any number of other functions, and those called function can further call other functions. The first section in the *main()* function, as well as other functions, contains local declarations. These declarations are local in the sense that they pertain to the requirements of that function only. The second section in the *main()* function, as well as in other functions, contains the statements that defines the actions to be performed by the function.

Section 5 is also optional. If present, it contains the other functions.

Note: *If the problem to be solved is simple and small in size, then only the main() function is sufficient to accomplish the task. However, if the problem is complex and the size of the problem is large, it is divided into small and independent subproblems, and then we write separate functions for each subproblem. The main() function coordinates the execution of these functions by appropriate calls to these functions, and synthesizes the solutions of the subproblems obtained from these functions.*

Question #5

What are various forms that *main()* function can take?

Answer

The *main()* function is a part of every C program. The C language permits following forms of *main()* function:

- `main()`
- `main(void)`
- `void main()`
- `int main()`

- `void main(void)`
- `int main(void)`

The empty pair of parenthesis indicates that the *main()* function takes no arguments. This may be explicitly indicated by using the keyword *void* inside the parenthesis.

We may also specify the keyword *void* or *int* before the word main.

When the keyword *void* is used, it indicates that the function *main()* does not return any value to the operating system.

When the keyword *int* is used, it indicates that the function *main()* will return an integer value to the operating system. Value 0 is returned to the operating system to indicate that the program terminated on completion of its intended task whereas the value 1 is used to indicate that the program terminated prematurely (could not complete its intended task).

Question #6

What are the steps in building a C program?

Answer

Once the design of the program is ready, the next step is to convert the program design into a computer program. During this conversion each of the steps of the program design is coded as one or more C language instructions. Here also it is recommended that one should write the program first on a piece of paper before keying in the computer.

Creating and Editing Programs

Once the program is ready on paper, we key in computer memory using a *text editor.* A text editor helps us to enter the character data into computer memory, allows editing (changing) the data in computer memory, and save the data from memory in a disk file on secondary memory with extension ".*c*".

This stored file is known as *source file*, and its contents are known as *source code.* This source file will be the input for the compiler.

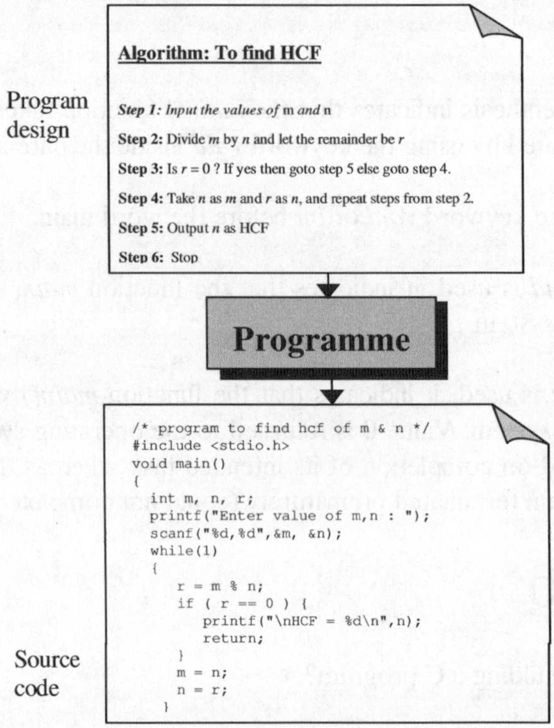

Figure 3.2: Program creation process

The programmer must carefully follow the language rules, which precisely specify how to express certain operations. Violation of language rules results in grammatical errors, more precisely known as *syntax errors*. Program development tool - *Compiler*, will check these syntax errors. These syntax errors must be eliminated before moving further.

Compiling Programs

The source code in the source file, stored on the disk, must to be translated into machine language. This job is done by the *compiler*. The C compiler actually is a combination of two separate programs – the *preprocessor* and the *translator*.

The *preprocessor* reads the source code and prepares it for translation. While reading the source code, it scans the code for preprocessor directives and processes them accordingly. For example, when it encounters the *include* directive, it substitutes that directive with the contents of the specified header file (such as *stdio.h*), and when it encounters the *define* directive, it substitutes the identifier with the specified literal (constant). The output from the preprocessor is an intermediate file, known as *translation unit*.

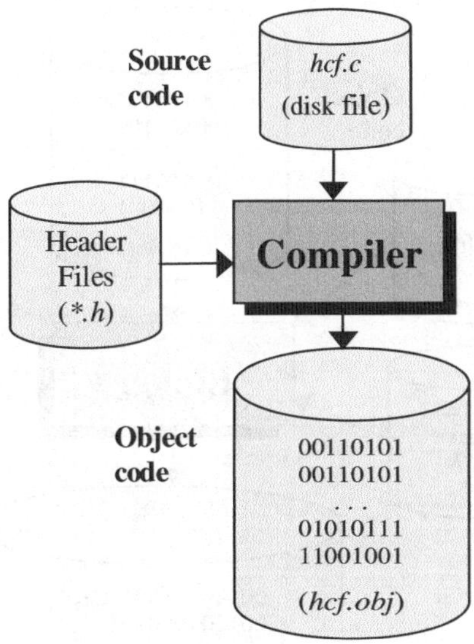

Figure 3.3: Compilation process

The translator reads the translation unit instruction-by-instruction and checks them for their grammatical accuracy. If there is any syntax error in it, it flags an error message – called *diagnostic message* on the screen. These diagnostics messages help the programmer to identify the cause of the syntax error and the place where it is present.

Therefore, if there is even a single syntax error, the translation process, known as *compilation*, is terminated. In that case, open the source file using the text editor, and make the necessary corrections and repeat the compilation.

However, if there are no syntax errors in the translation unit, the translator rereads the instruction from the beginning, translates them into machine language, and writes them onto a disk file. The translated version of the source code is known as *object code*, and is stored in the disk file with extension "**.obj*".

Linking Programs

Once the source code is translated into object code, though it is in machine language, still it is not in executable form. The reason being is that it may be referring to other functions which are not included in the object code. These referred functions can be library functions (pre-written functions supplied with the compiler in the form of libraries) or user-defined functions stored in other source files and which are compiled separately. All these functions also need to be included in the object code to get a final machine code which is in the executable form, known as *executable code*. This task is performed by the *linker*.

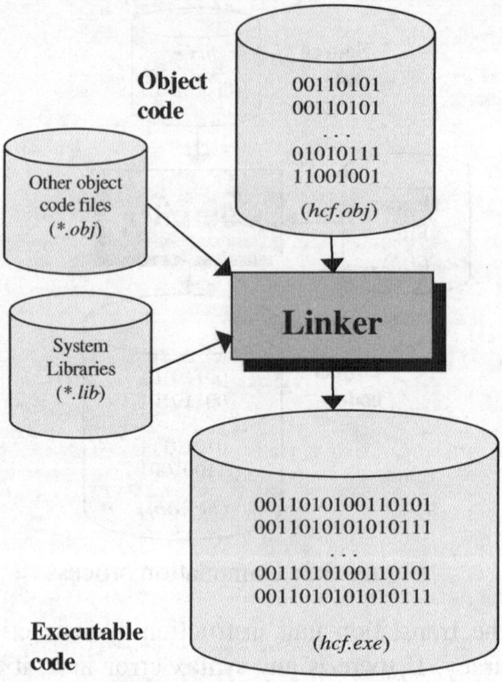

Figure 3.4: Linking process

A *linker* is a development tool that extracts the referred library functions from the system libraries, reads the object codes of the user-defined functions from the object files and integrates them with the current object code to produce the final executable code, which is stored in disk file with extension "*.*exe*". This executable code is the final form of the program that is ready for execution.

Executing Programs

Once the program is linked, it is ready for execution. To execute a program we give an operating system command, such as *run*, to load the program into computer memory and execute it. Getting the program into memory is the function of an operating system program known as *loader*. The loader locates the executable program in the secondary storage, reads it and brings into the computer memory. Once the program is loaded, the operating system transfers the control to the program and the program begins its execution.

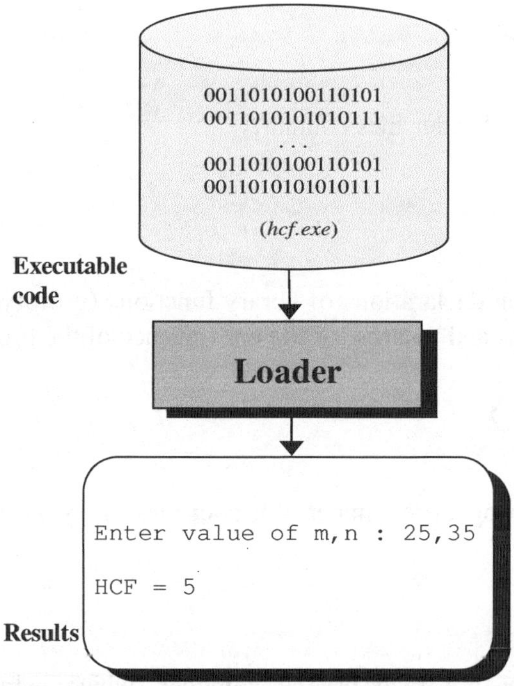

Figure 3.5: Program execution

Question #7

The output produced by a C compiler is an object code, *i.e.*, machine code, but not in a form that can be executed. Why?

Answer

Recall that a program can contain calls to library function as well as user-defined functions that are in other disk files and are not included using *file inclusion* preprocessor directive (*#include*).

The compiler doesn't have access to the definitions of these functions, and hence can't bind the function calls to function definitions. Hence, function calls are left unresolved. In addition, some more information is required by the operating system to run the program.

Question #8

Basically, what does the header files contain?

Answer

The header files contain declarations of library functions (prototypes of library functions) and useful enumerations and macros for the convenience of the programmers.

Question #9

What is the need of having large number of header files? Why not just one?

Answer

Note that header files are read by the compiler, which helps it in the process of compilation of the program. If all header files are combined into a single header file, this file will become very large and lot of compiler's time will be wasted. Further, note that in a program, we are not going to use diverse library functions in a single program, hence relevant declarations are put in different header files and relevant and meaningful names are given to these header files that show its intent.

Question #10

What is the difference between #include <...> and # include "..."?

Answer

There are two ways to include a header file:

```
#include <stdio.h>      and      #include "stdio.h"
```

The first form directs the preprocessor to include the header file from the standard directory while the second form directs the preprocessor to look for the specified header file in the user directory.

Question #11

What happens during linking?

Answer

The next step after compilation is linking, *i.e.*, to resolve the unresolved references to functions. This task is accomplished by another program known as *linker*. The linker takes object code(s) as its inputs and searches for unresolved references. For every unresolved reference, it searches libraries for their definitions and adds them to the end of final code being generated and fills its address at point of call. If search of any function is unsuccessful, the linker will generate a message like unresolved references and the also gives the name of the function called. The output of a linker is a machine language program that is in executable form better known as executable code or run file.

Question #12

What is the difference between declaration and definition of a variable?

Answer

Declaration only identifies the data type of a variable whereas definition causes the space to be reserved for the variable. Thus, declaration is a place where the nature of the variable is stated but no storage is allocated whereas definition is the place where the variable is created or assigned storage.

Question #13

What is the difference between the following statements?

```
extern int k;      and      int k;
```

Answer

The first is a declaration indicated that *k* is a variable of type *int* and is defined externally, *i.e.*, in some another source file. The second is a definition and causes 2-bytes to be reserved for it.

Question #14

What is the restriction on the declarations and/or definitions of variables?

Answer

The restriction on the declarations and/or definitions is that they must come before the executable statements in a block, and hence they appear in the beginning of a block.

Question #15

Suppose a global variable and a local variable have the same name. Is it possible to access a global variable from a block where local variable is defined?

Answer

No. It is not possible in C. It is always the most local variable that gets preference.

Question #16

Differentiate between local and global variables?

Answer

Local	Global
❑ These variables only exist inside the specific function that creates them. ❑ They are unknown to other functions and to the main program. ❑ Local variables are allocated memory on the stack and they cease to exist once the function that created them has completed execution. ❑ They are recreated each time a function is executed or called. Local variables are not initialized automatically. ❑ Their scope and life is limited to the function in which they are declared.	❑ These variables can be accessed by any function contained in the program. ❑ These variables are visible throughout the program from the point of their declaration. ❑ They do not get recreated if the function is called. ❑ To declare a global variable, declare it outside all the functions. ❑ If the local variable is declared with same name as a global variable, then the function will use the local variable that was declared within it and ignore the global variable. ❑ Global variables are declared to 0 by default. ❑ Global variables are allocated memory on the data segment.

Question #17

Write a "hello world" program in C without using a semicolon.

Answer

```
#include<stdio.h>
void main()
{
    if ( printf("hello world\n") ) { }
}
```

Explanation: The *printf*() is a function that returns the number of characters it is able to print. This return value can be used in the *if* conditional expression. With this combination, we can print the required string without using a semicolon.

Question #18

What is the difference between static and global variables?

Answer

While the life of an object determines whether the object is still in the memory (of the process), scope of the object decides whether the variable can be accessed at that point in the program. Static variables are local in scope to the block or file in which they are defined, but their lifespan is throughout the program. For instance, a static variable inside a function cannot be called from outside the function (because it's not in the scope) but is alive and exists in the memory. It retains its old value between function calls.

Global variables persist throughout the program; scope is also throughout the program. It means that global variables can be accessed from any function, any file (unless declared static) in the program.

Question #19

What is the use of *register* keyword in the context of variables?

Answer

The register keyword specifies that the variable is to be stored in the CPU register, if possible. Variables are usually stored in stack and passed to and from the computer processor, as and when required, the speed the data is sent at is pretty but can be improved on. Almost all computer processors contain CPU registers, these are memory slots on the actual processors, and storing data there gets rid of the overhead of the retrieving data from the stack. This memory (in registers) is quite small compared to normal memory, therefore, only a few variables can be stored there. Having a register keyword for variables and parameters also reduces code size, which is important in embedded systems. The number of available CPU registers is strictly dependent on the architectural design of the CPU itself. The number of CPU registers is 32 in most cases.

Question #20

How do we make a global variable accessible across files? Explain the *extern* keyword.

Answer

If a variable is declared (with global scope) in one file but referenced in other, the extern keyword is used to inform the compiler of variable's existence. Note that the keyword extern is for declarations, not definitions. An extern declaration does not create any storage. Variable initializations should not be done with extern.

Question #21

What is a function prototype?

Answer

A function prototype is a declaration similar to variable declarations. Function declarations are generally placed in header files. Specifically, it tells the compiler

- The name of the function
- The type of the output returned by the function.
- The number of types of inputs (called arguments), if any, the function expects to receive and the order in which it expects to receive them.

Question #22

What is the difference between declaration and definition of a function?

Answer

Like variables, declaration of a function only identifies the return type of the function and the type of format arguments. The declaration of a function is usually referred as a *function prototype*. On the other hand, definition of a function contains the statements to accomplish the intended task. Like variables, functions also have an address associated with its name.

Question #23

What does keyword *extern* mean in a function declaration?

Answer

Use the extern modifier in a method declaration to indicate that the method is implemented externally. Similarly, when you declare a variable as extern your program doesn't actually reserve any memory for it; extern emphasizes that the variable already exists external to the function or file. If you want to make a variable available to every file in every project you declare it globally in one file, that is, not inside any function, and add an extern declaration of that variable to a header file that is included in all the other files.

Question #24

How do you access command line arguments?

Answer

A program is started by the operating system by calling a program's *main*() function. The *main*() function is the only function in C that can be defined in multiple ways. It can take no arguments, two arguments, or three arguments. The two and three argument forms allow it to receive arguments from the shell. The two arguments takes an int and an array of strings. When defining *main*() function any name can be given but it is convention to call them *argc* and *argv*[]. The first argument (*argc*) holds a count of how many elements there are in the array of strings passed as the second argument (*argv*). The array is always null terminated so *argv* [*argc*] = null.

Here's short program demonstrating the use:

```
int main (int argc, char *argv[])
{
    int i;
    for( i = 0; i< argc; i++ ) {
        printf("argv[%d] == %s\n", i, argv[i]);
    }
    return 0;
}
```

The integer *argc* is the argument count (hence *argc*). It is the number of arguments passed into the program from the command line, including the name of the program.

The array of character pointers is the listing of all the arguments. The *argv*[0] is the name of the program. After that every element number less than *argc* is command line arguments. You can use each *argv* element just like a string, or *argv* as a two dimensional array.

Question #25

What will the output of the following program?

```
1:  void main()
2:  {
3:      int intVar = 20;
4:      printf("\n%d, %d, %d\n",
5:          intVar==20, intVar=35, intVar<50);
6:  }
```

Answer

0, 35, 1

Explanation: Recall that the arguments to a function are passed from right-to-left.

Therefore, in a call to *printf()* function in line number 3, first expression "intVar<50" is evaluated which results in value 1 since the value of *intVar* variable is 20 which is less than 50.

Next expression "intVar=35" statement is executed that causes value 35 to be assigned to *intVar* variable.

Finally, expression "intVar==20" is evaluated which result in value 0 since the value of *intVar* variable is 35 which is not equal to 20.

Question #26

Find the error(s), if any, in the following program

```
1:  void main()
2:  {
3:     float a, b;
4:     printf( "\nEnter value of a: " );
5:     scanf( "%f", a );
6:     b = a * 3;
7:     printf( "\nValue of b = %f\n", b );
8:  }
```

Answer

Error *Address of* (&) operator missing before variable *a* in a call to *scanf()* function in line number 5.

Question #27

What will the output of the following program?

```
1:  void main()
2:  {
3:    int x;
4:      x = 0x10 + 10 + 010;
5:      printf("\nx = %d\n", x);
6:  }
```

Answer

x = 34

Explanation: In line number 3, right hand side is an expression "0x10+10+010" which stands for sum of three integer numbers – hexadecimal number 0x10 which is equivalent to decimal number 16, decimal number 10 and octal number 010 which is equivalent to decimal number 8.

Hence, the expression "0x10 + 10 + 010" is evaluated as an expression "16 + 10 + 8" which is equal to 34.

Question #28

What will the output of the following program?

```
void main()
{
   printf(" %d\n", printf("\nBalle Balle"));
}
```

Answer

Balle Balle 12

Explanation: Recall that printf() function returns number of character position displayed. Since the second argument to the printf() function is another call to printf() function, so inner call will be executed first. This output string "Balle Balle" and return value 12, since it has displayed 12 characters and then this value is printed by the outer call. Hence the output "Balle Balle 12".

Question #29

What will be the output of the following program, if we give value 200 for *j* and 50 for *k*?

```
void main()
{
    int j, k;
    printf( "\nItems read = %d\n",
              scanf("%d,%d", &j, &k));
    printf("\nj = %d, k = %d\n", j, k);
}
```

Answer

Items read = 2

j = 200, k = 50

Explanation: Recall that *scanf()* function returns the number of items read. Since, we have entered two values therefore, the *scanf()* function returns value 2.

Question #30

What will be the output of the following program?

```
int sum(int,int,int); /*function prototype*/
void main()
{
    int a = 10;
    printf( “\nValue returned by function” );
    printf( “ = %d\n”, sum(a++, ++a, ++a) );
}
int sum( int a, int b, int c )
{
  return (a+b+c);
}
```

Answer

Value returned by function = 35

Explanation: Since arguments are passed right-to-left to a function, hence the function call “sum(a++, ++a, ++a)” becomes a function call “sum(12, 12, 11)”.

Question #31

Is the name of the formal arguments in a function prototype mandatory?

Answer

No. Only data type is mandatory. However, the name of formal arguments can be useful to know the kind of arguments that a function will be taking. This is explained with the help of the following example:

The *displayAt()*function accepts three arguments: row number, column number, and a string. It display the string starting from the given row and column.

The prototype of this function can be

```
void displayAt(int, int, char *);
```

But from this prototype, it is not clear whether row is to passed as first argument or column is to be passed as first argument. However, if its prototype is taken as

```
void displayAt(int row, int col, char *charPtr);
```

then it is clear that first argument will be row while the second will be column.

Question #32

What is the significance of storage class?

Answer

The storage class, in general, determines the scope and lifetime of a variable, which in turn helps to economize the memory usage.

Question #33

What is the difference between the following declarations?

```
const int *intptr;

int *const intptr;
```

Answer

First one is pointer to a constant *int*, while the second one is constant pointer to *int*.

Question #34

What is the difference between the following declarations?

```
int *ptr(int arg);

int (*ptr)(int arg);
```

Answer

First is the prototype of a function that takes an integer argument, and returns a pointer to an integer. Second one is declaration of a pointer to a function that takes an integer argument and returns an integer.

Question #35

What is the difference between the following declarations?

```
int (*a)[];
int *a[];
```

Answer

First one indicates a pointer to an array of integers, whereas the second one indicates an array of pointers to integers.

Question #36

How will you interpret the following declaration?

```
int *(*ptr)(int (*a)[]);
```

Answer

Since *(*ptr)(. . .)* indicates a pointer to a function, therefore, *int *(*ptr)(. . .)* indicates a pointer to a function that returns a pointer to an integer. Now within the last pair of parenthesis, *int (*a)[]* indicates a pointer to an array of integers. Therefore, putting pieces together, *int *(*ptr)(int (*a)[])* indicates a pointer to a function that takes a pointer to an array of integers as an argument and returns a pointer to an array.

Question #37

What is a dangling pointer?

Answer

It is a pointer that is not initialized with a valid address. Such a pointer can end up pointing anywhere in memory that may include the program code itself or to the code of the operating system. The use of such pointer can lead to undesirable results. Therefore, care must be taken to initialize pointers with valid address before use.

Question #38

What is a memory leak?

Answer

It is a situation where the programmer fails to release the memory allocated at run time in a module. Remember that when memory is allocated, a pointer variable is used to hold the address of the allocated block, however, when the module completes its execution, the pointer variable goes out of scope and there will be no way to reach that memory block. Therefore, care must be taken to release the allocated memory block in a module where memory was allocated.

Question #39

What is a NULL pointer assignment?

Answer

It is a situation that happens when a pointer points to address 0, which is called NULL. For example, it may happen that if the pointer variable is declared as global, since global variables are initialized to 0. Likewise, this can also happen for a local un-initialized pointer variable, particularly for local static variables, they are also initialized to 0. When it happens, and the pointer is used on the left-hand side of an assignment operator, the system generates a message "*Null pointer assignment*".

Question #40

What is an allocation failure?

Answer

It is a situation when the program through *malloc()*, *calloc()*, or *realloc()* function request for a block of memory, and the operating could not fulfill the request of the program because the sufficient memory may not be available in the free pool. In that case, these functions return a NULL pointer indicating the allocation failure. Therefore, the programmer should take care of allocation failures and provide a safe exit in their programs on such failures.

Question #41

What will be the output of the following program?

```
1:  void main()
2:  {
3:      float x = 1 / 2.0 - 1 / 2;
4:      printf( "%.2f", x );
5:  }
```

Answer

0.50

Explanation: First expression (1/2.0) will be evaluated. Here, nominator is an integer operand and the denominator is a real (float) operand, therefore the integer operand will be converted to real operands and then real division is performed yielding 0.5.

Next expression (1/2) will be evaluated. Here, nominator and denominator both are integer operands; therefore the integer division is performed yielding 0.

Hence, value of expression on right hand side of the assignment statement in line 3 is 0.5.

Question #42

Is there any error in the following function?

```
myFunction( a + b, c, d, 5 )
int a, b, c, d;
{
    int sum;
    sum = a + b + c + d + 5;
    return sum;
}
```

Answer

Yes, because expressions and constants are not permitted as arguments.

Question #43

What will be the output of the following program?

```
1:  void main()
2:  {
3:      int i;
4:      int a[] = { 5, 7, 9, 11, 13 };
5:      for ( i = 0; i <=4; i++ )
6:      {
7:          if ( i )
8:              continue;
9:          else
10:             printf( "%5d", i[a] );
11:     }
12: }
```

Answer

5

Explanation: First thing to note is that if *a* is an one-dimensional array, its *i*th element can be accessed as *a*[*i*] or *i*[*a*] using subscript notation. Both are valid since during the compilation, the compiler will convert them as *(*a*+*i*) and *(*i*+*a*), which are equivalent.

Further note that the *for* loop in line 5 will execute for values $i =$ 0, 1, 2, 3, 4. Within the body of the loop, there is a if statement at line 7 with variable *i* as its condition. We know that zero value is equivalent to boolean false and non-zero value is equivalent true. Thus, for $i = 0$, the condition fails and for all other values holds. Further, when condition fails, else part is executed otherwise if part is executed which contains *continue* statement and its execution terminates the current iteration.

Thus, *printf()* function will be called only once and that is when $i = 0$, hence it will output *i*[0], *i.e.*, 5 only in five column space.

Question #44

What do you mean by *Lvalue* and *Rvalue*?

Answer

There are two values associated with a variable:

1. Its data value that is stored at some memory address. This sometimes referred to as variable's *Rvalue* (pronounced as "are-value"). We may think *Rvalue* as meaning *read value*. Both a literal constant and a variable can serve as *rvalue*.
2. Its address value that is its address in memory within which its data value is stored. This sometimes referred to as variable's *Lvalue* (pronounced as "ell-value"). We may think *Lvalue* as meaning *location value*. Only a variable can serve as *Lvalue*.

Question #45

What will be the output of the following program?

```
#define A 1
#define C 3
void main()
{
    #ifdef A
        printf(“10”);
    #endif
    #ifdef C
        printf(“20”)
    #endif
    #ifndef B
        printf(“30”);
    #endif
}
```

Answer

102030

Explanation: Since it contains conditional directives, the preprocessor will produce the following intermediate program:

```
void main()
{
    printf(“10”);
    printf(“20”)
    printf(“30”);
}
```

which is then compiled by the compiler. I think, now you can understand what the output will be.

Question #46

Which would be the output of the following program?

```
void main()
{
    int a[5] = { 1, 2 };
    printf("\n%d,%d,%d\n", a[2], a[3], a[4]);
}
```

Answer

0, 0, 0

Explanation: Note that array is partially initialized, *i.e.*, only first two elements are initialized. Thus, *a*[0] and *a*[1] are initialized with value 1 and 2, respectively. *What about a[2], a[3], a[4]?* They all are initialized to 0, as the remaining elements of partially filled array are always initialized to value 0.

Question #47

What will the output of the following program?

```
1:  void main()
2:  {
3:     int *p, a[] = { 1, 2, 3, 4, 5 };
4:     p = &a[2];
5:     cout << p[-1];
6:  }
```

Answer

2

Explanation: In line number 4, address of element *a*[2], *i.e.*, value 3, is assigned to pointer variable *p*. In line number 5, expression *p*[-1] is equivalent to *(*p*-1). Note that subtracting 1 from pointer variable *p* giving address of preceding element, *i.e.*, 2, and hence the output.

Question #48

What will be the output of the following program?

```
1:  void main()
2:  {
3:      int i = -3, j = 2, k = 0, m;
4:      m = ++i && j++ && ++k;
5:      printf("\n%d, %d, %d, %d\n", i, j, k, m);
6:  }
```

Answer

–2, 3, 1, 1

Explanation: In a logical expression, if the first operand determines the outcome of the expression then the second operand is not evaluated. In line number 4, the expression "++i && j++ && ++k" will be evaluated as "((++i && j++) && ++k)" as illustrated below:

First variable *i* is incremented and since new value of *i* is –2 (non-zero), it alone cannot determine the outcome; therefore the second operand is evaluated. Next, current value of *j* (which is 2) is used and then incremented. Since current value is non-zero, the outcome of sub expression "(++i && j++)" is 1 (non-zero), and new value of *j* is 3. Since, the above sub expression cannot determine the outcome of the expression, the next operand is evaluated. Hence *k* is incremented and since new value of *k* is 1 (non-zero), therefore the outcome of entire expression is 1, and finally the value of expression (which is 1) is assigned to 1.

Thus, after completion of the instruction in line number 4, the value of *i* = -2, *j* = 3, *k* = 1, and *m* = 1, and hence the output.

Question #49

What will be the output of the following program?

```
void main()
{
    const int i = 5;
    int *p;
    i = 20;
    p = &i;
    printf(“\n%d, %d\n”, *p, i);
}
```

Answer

It will give a compile time error in line number 5, because variable *i* is declared as constant and thus the modification of value of *i* is not permitted.

Question #50

What will be the output of the following program?

```
1:  #define  EVEN(x)    x % 2 ? 1 : 0
2:  void main()
3:  {
4:      int a = 5;
5:      if ( EVEN(a + 1) )
6:          printf( "\n%d is even\n", a + 1 );
7:      else
8:          printf( "\n%d is odd\n", a + 1 );
9:  }
```

Answer

6 is even

Explanation: After preprocessing, contents of intermediate file will be as shown below:

```
1:  void main()
2:  {
3:      int a = 5;
4:      if ( a + 1 % 2 ? 1 : 0 )
6:          printf( "\n%d is even\n", a + 1 );
7:      else
8:          printf( "\n%d is odd\n", a + 1 );
9:  }
```

This file goes as input to the compiler. From the above code you can judge that the conditional expression of *if* statement always evaluates to value 1, hence always *printf()* function in line 6 is invoked.

Question #51

Is any thing wrong with the following declaration?

```
int k = 1+2+3;
```

Answer

No. Remember that all constant expressions are evaluated by the compiler. Hence, above declaration statement will be treated as “`int k = 6;`” before compilation.

Question #52

Is any thing wrong with the following program?

```
void main()
{
  int i = 2, j = 3, k;
  scanf(“%d”, &k);
  switch(k)
  {
    case i:
       printf(“Values of k is 2”);
       break;
    case j:
       printf(“Values of k is 3”);
       break;
    default:
       printf(“Values of k is other ”);
       printf(“than 2 or 3”);
  }
}
```

Answer

Yes. Variables cannot be used as case values.

Question #53

Cite some cases where *switch* statement cannot be used?

Answer

The *switch* statement cannot be used when the variable or expression is not of integral type (*int*, *long* or *char*). The other situation is where conditions are of type that does not require exact match, such *amount* <= 1200.

Question #54

Consider the following statement

```
a <= 20 ? b = 30: c = 30;
```

This statement assigns value 30 to *b* if the value of *a* is less than or equal to 20 otherwise assigns value 30 to *c*.

Is there any way of rewriting the above statement so that value 30 is used only once?

Answer

Yes. It can be done as follows:

```
*((a <= 20) ? &b: &c) = 30;
```

Explanation

Here, if the condition is true, then value of conditional expression will be the address of variable *b* else address of variable *c*, then value 30 is assigned to that address.

Question #55

What will be the output of the following program?

```
void main()
{
  long a = 15;
  int i;
  char *p;
  p = (char *) &a;
  for ( i = 0; i <= 3; i++ )
    printf("%02X ", p[i]);
}
```

Answer

0F 00 00 00

Explanation: Note that integer number 15 as *long* integer will be represented as string of 32 bits as 0000 0000 0000 000F. Further, note that on Intel processors it will be stored as 000F 0000 0000 0000 starting from lower address to higher address. The address of the location is always the address of first byte. Hence, when we make an attempt to access this number using *char* pointer, we will be able to access the contents of individual bytes, and hence the output.

Question #56

What will be the output of the following program?

```
 1:  void main()
 2:  {
 3:      int sumOfDigits(int);
 4:      int a, b;
 5:      a = sumOfDigits(125);
 6:      b = sumOfDigits(125);
 7:      printf("%d, %d", a, b);
 8:  }
 9:  int sumOfDigits(int n)
10:  {
11:      static int sum = 0;
12:      while ( n > 0 )
13:      {
14:        sum += n % 10;
15:        n /= 10;
16:      }
17:      return sum;
18:  }
```

Answer

8, 16

Explanation: You may be expecting answer "8, 8" since we are attempting to find the sum of digits of same number 125.

Look at line number 11, the local variable *sum* is declared with *static* storage class. Further, lifetime of a static variable is program execution time, hence a static variable is able to retain its existing value between different calls. Therefore, on the first call, the *sum* variable is initialized to 0 and at return time has value 8. In the second call, the initial value of *sum* is 8, and further 8 (sum of digits of 125) is added thus giving value 16.

Question #57

Is there any difference between expressions "*ptr++" and "++*ptr"?

Answer

Yes. The first expression accesses the contents of the current location and then increments the pointer whereas the second expression increments the contents of the current location.

Question #58

Can you write an expression equivalent to "++*ptr"?

Answer

Yes. It is "(*ptr)++".

Question #59

Consider the following program

```
 1:  void main()
 2:  {
 3:      int *p;
 4:      void fun(. . .);
 5:      /*  some code here    */
 6:      fun(&p);
 7:      /* some more code here  */
 8:  }
 9:  void fun(. . .)
10:  {
11:      /* some code here */
18:  }
```

Complete the instructions at line number 4 and 9.

Answer

```
4:   void fun(int **);
9:   void fun(int **q)
```

Explanation: Note that in the function call, we are passing the address of a pointer variable; therefore the corresponding formal argument should be a pointer to a pointer.

This situation can be better understood by considering the call by reference mechanism. If we pass address of normal variable, then corresponding formal argument is a pointer, if we pass address of a pointer variable, then formal argument should be a pointer to a pointer, and if you we pass address of a pointer to a pointer, then formal argument should be pointer to a pointer to a pointer.

Question #60

What will be the output of the following program?

```
1:  void main()
2:  {
3:      char str1[] = “Hello World”;
4:      char str2[] = “Hello World”;
5:      if ( str1 == str2 )
6:          printf(“Strings are equal”);
7:      else
8:          printf(“Strings are unequal”);
9:  }
```

Answer

Strings are unequal

Explanation: Note that although both the strings are identical, but they are stored in different sections of memory, and hence the pointer *str1* and *str2* contain different addresses. In line number 5, pointers are compared and since pointers are unequal, the *else* part of the *if* statement is executed.

Question #61

Is there any error in the following program?

```
1:  #include <stdio.h>
2:  void main()
3:  {
4:     int c;
5:     printf( “\nEnter value of c: ” );
6:     scanf( “%d", &c);
7:     switch(c);
8:     {
9:        case 1 : printf(“\nHello 1\n”);
10:                break;
11:       case 2 : printf(“\nHello 2\n”);
12:                break;
13:      default : printf(“\nInvaild value\n”);
14:                break;
15:       case 3 : printf(“\nHello 3\n”);
16:                break;
17:       case 4 : printf(“\nHello 4\n”);
18:    }
19: }
```

Answer

Yes. Note that in line 7, there is semicolon, which terminates the *switch* statement. Further, the *case* keyword can only be used in the block of *switch* statement, therefore, the compiler will flash the error message “Case outside of switch statement in function main” followed “Misplaced break in function main” for all cases and the *break* statements.

Question #62

Among *gets()* and *fgets()* functions, which function is safe to use?

Answer

fgets() is safe to use. This is illustrated below. The prototype of *gets()* functions is

```
char *gets(char *s);
```

It reads a string of characters terminated by newline characters from *stdin* and stores in s. As there is no way to tell the size of the string there is always a possibility of overflow.

The prototype of *fgets()* functions is

```
char *gets(char *s, int n, FILE *stream);
```

It reads a string of characters from *stream* and stores in *s*. It stops when either it reads (*n*-1) characters or a newline character, whichever comes first. So overflow condition never occurs.

Question #63

Find out the error, if any, in the following program. Here file named *mydata.dat* contains a list of strings.

```
#include <stdio.h>
void main()
{
   FILE *fptr;
   char str[80];
   fptr = fopen(“c:\tc\mydata.dat”, “r”);
   while ( fgets(str, 80, fptr) != NULL)
       puts(str);
   fclose(fptr);
}
```

Answer

The path of file should be “c:\\tc\\mydata.dat”.

Question #64

What will be the output of the following program?

```
#include <stdio.h>
void main()
{
   int i, j = 10;
   i = j + NULL;
   printf("\ni = %d\n", i);
}
```

Answer

i = 10

Explanation: Note that NULL is defined as macro with value 0 in header file named *stdio.h*.

Question #65

Find out the error, if any, in the following program.

```
 1:  #include <stdio.h>
 2:  void main()
 3:  {
 4:      int a = 10, *i;
 5:      void *j;
 6:      i = j = &a;
 7:      i++;
 8:      j++;
10:      printf("\n%u %u\n", i, j);
11:  }
```

Answer

Error will be reported in line 8 and the compiler will give message something like "Size of the type is unknown". The reason is that on *void* (*generic*) *pointers*, arithmetic operations are not permitted unless appropriately typecasted.

Question #66

What will be the output of the following program?

```
#include <stdio.h>
void main()
{
    int a = 10, b = 20, c = 5, d;
    d = a < b < c;
    printf("\nd = %d\n", d);
}
```

Answer

i = 1

Explanation: Note that expression "a < b < c" will be evaluated as "(a<b) < c". Since a < b, thus it gives value 1 and further 1 < 5, it gives 1, and hence the output.

Question #67

What will be the output of the following program if we enter the string "Hello brother"?

```
#include <stdio.h>
void main()
{
    char str[20];
    printf("\nEnter any string = ");
    scanf("%s", str);
    printf("\nInput string is %s\n", str);
}
```

Answer

Input String is Hello

Explanation: The format specifier "%s" in *scanf()* function can only be used to input a single word string. The space after world Hello will be treated as string terminator. Therefore, the rest of the string is ignored and is left in the keyboard buffer.

Question #68

What will be the output of the following program if we enter the string "Hello brother"?

```
#include <stdio.h>
void main()
{
    char str[20];
    printf("\nEnter any string = ");
    scanf("%[^\n]", str);
    printf("\nInput string is %s\n", str);
}
```

Answer

Input String is Hello brother

Explanation: The format specifier "%[^\n]" in *scanf()* function is used to input a multiword string. The input is completed when newline character is encountered.

Question #69

Does reading a string using *scanf()* cause overflow?

Answer

Yes. Like *gets()* function, there is no way to tell *scanf()* function about the maximum size of the array for input string.

Question #70

What would be the consequence if the function prototypes are local to *main()* function?

Answer

If any other function calls these functions, the compiler will flag an error message, as these prototypes are not available in that function, hence the compiler may not be able to compile the program properly.

Question #71

When should the function prototypes be made global?

Answer

When the functions can be called from more than one function.

Question #72

Is the following nested comments are acceptable?

```
/*  Outer comment  /* Nested comments */ allowed/not allowed */
```

Answer

No. Note that anything that lies between /* and */ is treated as comment. Therefore, in the above case, from word *Outer* to word *comments* everything is treated as comment including /*. Hence the string "allowed/not allowed */" does not lie in the comment.

Thus, it is being improper statement the compiler will flag an error.

Question #73

When should we pass arguments by reference (address)?

Answer

Argument passing by reference (address) is useful in following situations:

- When we intend to change the values of actual arguments.
- When we want to save the memory by preventing the creation of large array and/or structure variables being passed to the function.

Question #74

Given a choice, would you prefer to use *const* over *#define* preprocessor in order to use a constant?

Answer

Using *const* is always a better choice because we can control its scope, which is not possible with *#define*.

Question #75

Passing arguments by reference (address), we can prevent the creation of large array and/or structure variables in the called function. Here the called function can change the values of array and/or structure variables. Is there any way to prevent the called function from doing so?

Answer

Yes, by prefixing the formal argument by keyword *const* as shown in the following example

```
void fName(const int *a)
{
   /*    some statements    */
}
```

Question #76

In the following declarations, which is constant and which is variable?

```
char *charPtr = "Sample string";
const char *charPtr = "Sample string";
char const *charPtr = "Sample string";
char * const charPtr = "Sample string";
const char * const charPtr = "Sample string";
```

Answer

In the first statement, both pointer and string are variables.

In the second statement, pointer is variable but string is constant.

In the third statement also, pointer is variable but string is constant.

In the fourth statement, pointer is constant but string is variable.

In the fifth statement, both pointer and string are constant.

Question #77

What are library functions? Where are they stored?

Answer

Library functions are a collection of predefined functions. They are stored in files with extension *lib*. These functions are shipped with the compiler for the convenience of the programmers.

Question #78

In how many ways can we pass arguments to a function?

Answer

There are two ways in which we can pass arguments to a function:

- By value

```
void f(int, int)  /* declaration  */
f(a, b);          /*  call   */
```

- By reference (address)

```
void f(int *, int *)  /* declaration  */
f(&a, &b);            /*  call   */
```

Question #79

Differentiate between call by value and call by reference (address).

Answer

Call by Value	Call by Reference (Address)
1. The actual arguments can be constants, variables, or expressions.	1. The actual arguments can only be variables.
2. The values of actual arguments are substituted in formal arguments which are ordinary variables.	2. The addresses of the actual arguments are substituted in formal arguments which are pointer variable.
3. Any change made to the formal arguments will have no effect on actual arguments, since the function will only be using the local copy of the arguments.	3. Any change made to the formal arguments will have immediate effect on actual arguments, since the function will be working on actual arguments through pointers.

Question #80

What are different file opening modes?

Answer

The following table shows the different file opening modes:

Table 5.1: File opening modes

Mode	Purpose
rt	Open a text file for reading. The file must already exist.
wt	Open a text file for writing. If the file already exists, its contents will be discarded. If it does not exist, it will be created.
at	Open a text file for extending. Data will be added to the end of the existing file, if file already exists. If it does not exist, it will be created.
rb	Open a binary file for reading. The file must already exist.
wb	Open binary file for writing. If the file already exists, its contents will be overwritten. If it does not exist, it will be created.
ab	Open binary file for extending. Data will be added to the end of the existing file, if file already exists. If it does not exist, it will be created.
rt+ or *r+t*	Open a text file for both reading and writing. The file must already exist.
wt+ or *w+t*	Open a text file for both reading and writing. If it does not exist, it will be created.
at+ or *a+t*	Open a text file for both reading and appending. If the file does not exist, it will be created.
rb+ or *r+b*	Open a binary file for both reading and writing. The file must already exist.
wb+ or *w+b*	Open a binary file for both reading and writing. If it does not exist, it will be created.
ab+ or *a+b*	Open a binary file for both reading and appending. If the file does not exist, it will be created.

Question #81

What is the purpose of *fseek()* function?

Answer

The *fseek()* function positions the file pointer at the specific location in the file. This position of the file pointer allows accessing the record in a random fashion.

Question #82

What is the purpose of *ftell()* function?

Answer

The *ftell()* function returns the current position of the file pointer in the file. If *ftell()* functions is used when the file pointer is at the end of the file, the number returned by *ftell()* gives the size of the file.

Question #83

Is it necessary to close the file and then open again if the file needs to be re-read in the same program?

Answer

No. The file pointer can be positioned at the beginning of the file either using *fseek()* function or the *rewind()* function.

Question #84

Write function call to *fseek()* function to position file pointer at the beginning of the file.

Answer

```
fseek(fptr, 0L, 0);
```

Question #85

Write the function call to *fseek()* function to position the file pointer at the end of the file.

Answer

```
fseek(fptr, 0L, 2);
```

Question #86

What is the difference between text mode and binary mode?

Answer

DIFFERENCES BETWEEN A TEXT FILE AND A BINARY FILE

Text File	Binary File
1. Data is stored using human readable characters.	1. Data is stored in the same format as it is stored in memory.
2. Each line of data ends with a *newline* character.	2. There are no lines or *newline* character.
3. There is a special character called end-of-file (EOF) marker at the end of the file.	3. There is an end-of-file marker at the end of the file, which is usually implementation dependent.

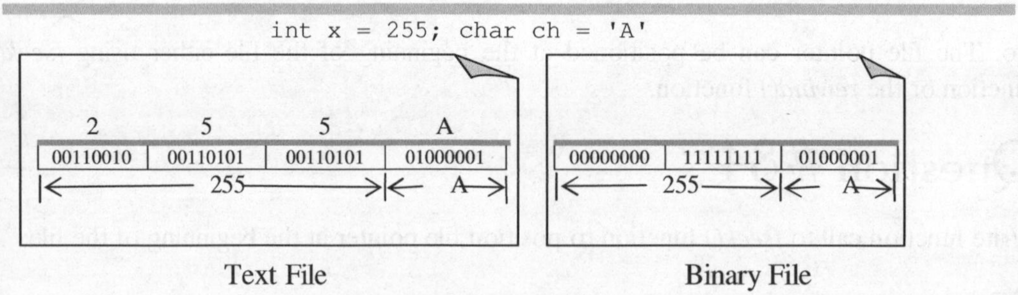

Figure 3.6: Text and Binary Files

Question #87

What is the main difference between *malloc()* and *calloc()*?

Answer

The main difference between *malloc()* and *calloc()* is that *malloc()* function just allocates the memory whereas the *malloc()* function also initializes the memory to zeros.

Question #88

What is free store/heap?

Answer

Free store/heap is area of memory from where memory is allocated at runtime using *malloc()* or *calloc()* functions.

Question #89

Consider the following statement

```
int intArray[] = { 0, 1, 2, 3, 4 };
```

Is there any difference between the expressions *intArray* and *&intArray*?

Answer

No. Both mean the same thing. Note that name of the array is the base address of the array and also it is the address of the first element of the array. And the expression *&intArray* is interpreted as *&intArray[0]*, which means the address of the first element of the array, and hence there is no difference between them.

Question #90

What will be the output of the following program?

```
1:  #include <stdio.h>
2:  #define MAX(a, b)    a > b ? b : a
3:  void main()
4:  {
5:      int max;
6:      max = MAX(2+3, 3+6);
7:      printf("%d", max);
8:  }
```

Answer

5

Explanation: After preprocessing, line 6 will expand to

```
max = 2+3 > 3+6 ? 3+6 : 2+3;
```

and since the condition is false, it takes second value, *i.e.*, 5.

Question #91

Is there any error in the following program?

```
#include <stdio.h>
#define MAX(a, b) =  a > b ? b : a;
void main()
{
    int max;
    max = MAX(2+3, 3+6);
    printf("%d", max);
}
```

Answer

Yes. The use of assignment operator and semicolon after the expression is not allowed.

Question #92

What are the differences between *exit()* and *return* statement?

Answer

- First difference is that *exit()* is a function while *return* is a statement.
- Second difference is that *exit()* function terminates the program while *return* statement terminate the function.
- Third difference is that *exit()* function always return some value where it is optional for *return* statement.

Question #93

Explain the usage of *atoi()*, *itoa()* and *gcvt()* functions.

Answer

These functions are declared in header file *stdlib.h.*

atoi() - Converts a string to an integer number.

```
int atoi(const char *str);
```

where *str* is a pointer to the string.

itoa() - Converts an integer number to a string. Its prototype is

```
char *itoa(int value, char *str, int radix);
```

where *value* is the integer number to be converted, *str* is pointer to character array where converted number is stored, and *radix* is base in which integer number is expressed.

gcvt() - Converts a floating-point number to a string. Its prototype is

```
char *itoa(double value, int ndec, char *str);
```

where *value* is the floating-number to be converted, *ndec* is the number of significant digits to be used, and *str* is pointer to character array where converted number is stored.

Question #94

Is there any way to convert a numerical value to a string?

Answer

Yes. Using *sprintf()* functions. The *sprintf()* function writes a string equivalent of a number into a character array. For example

```
char str[30];
float x = 250.25;
sprintf(str, "%.2f", x);
```

It writes the string equivalent of numerical value (with two decimal positions) into a character array named *str*.

Question #95

What is the difference between *rand()*, *random()*, *srand()*, and *randomize()*?

Answer

- *rand()* – returns successive pseudo random numbers in the range 0 to RAND_MAX.
- *random()* – returns random number between 0 and one less that its argument.
- *srand()* – initializes the random number generator with a given seed value.
- *randomize()* – initializes the random number generator with a random value.

Question #96

Without using redirection, how can you send the output of a program to a printer?

Answer

By using predefined name *stdprn* as file pointer for *fprintf()* function. The following statement will send the string "Hello" to the printer

```
fprintf(stdprn, "\n%s\n", "hello");
```

Question #97

Recall that when we use *free()* function to deallocate the block, we only pass pointer to the block, then how *free()* function know how many bytes it should deallocate?

Answer

When operating system allocates memory, on call to *malloc()*, *calloc()* or *realloc()* function, to a program from its free pool of memory (also called free store), it keeps track of the address of the block and the size of the block. Therefore, when the memory needs to be deallocated, program need only to tell the address of block to the operating system.

Question #98

Can we increase the size of the dynamically allocated array?

Answer

Yes. This can be done using the *realloc()* function.

Question #99

We can use *malloc()*, *calloc()* or *realloc()* functions to dynamically allocate in a program. Name the library functions needed to deallocate the memory allocated by these functions, respectively.

Answer

There is only one function named *free()* that is used to deallocate the memory allocated by above mentioned functions.

Question #100

Consider the following function definition. What can you say about it?

```
int fName(const int num)
{
        /*  some statements  */
}
```

Answer

There was no need to declare *num* as const since the argument passing by value prevents a function from modifying the value of *num*.

Question #101

What are the advantages of using *typedefs* in a program?

Answer

The advantages of using *typedefs* in a program are

- It makes writing of complicated declaration a lot easier, which in turn helps in eliminating lot of typographical errors.
- It also helps in achieving portability in programs. Suppose, there are some data types that are machine dependent and we use *typedefs* for those data types, then we only need to change *typedefs* as we move to new machine platform.

Question #102

You may have observed that when we use *scanf()* function to read the data for a field of type *float* of a structure, the system gives error message "Floating-point format not linked". What is the solution of this problem?

Answer

The possible solution of this problem is that you define a function in the program, where you assign the address of a variable of type *float* to a pointer also of type *float*. This will force the compiler to link the floating-point format, and hence problem will be solved. However, you don't need to call this function. Further, the name of function is immaterial.

The code of such a function may look like

```
void linkFloat(void)
{
    float a = 10, *b;
    b = &a;
}
```

Question #103

Why we need to explicitly typecast the pointer returned by the *malloc()*, *calloc()*, and *realloc()* functions when called to dynamically allocate memory?

Answer

Because these functions return a pointer of type *void* (generic pointer), it is always advisable to properly typecast the *void* pointer so that system behaves consistently.

Question #104

Write a recursive function to find sum of elements of an array named *a* with *n* elements.

Answer

```
int sum(int a[], int n)
{
   if ( n == 0 )
      return a[0];
   else
      return ( a[n-1] + sum(a,n-1) );
}
```

Question #105

What is self-referential structure?

Answer

If a structure contains a member that is a pointer to the same structure, then the structure is called self- referential structure.

```
struct list
{
   int nodedata;
   struct list *next;
};
```

Question #106

What is a void pointer?

Answer

When a variable is declared as being a pointer to a variable of type void it is known as a generic pointer. Since we cannot have a variable of type void, the pointer will not point to any data and therefore cannot be de-referenced. It is still a pointer though; to use it we have to cast it to another kind of pointer first. Hence, the term generic pointer.

This is very useful when you want a pointer to point to data of different types at different times. Here is an example code using a void pointer

```
void main()
{
    int i;
    char c;
    void *the_data;
    i = 7;
    c = 'a';
    the_data = &i;
    printf( "the_data points to integer value %d\n",
            *(int*)the_data);
    the _data = &c;
    printf("the_data now points to the character %c\n",
            *(char*)the_data);
}
```

Question #107

Why arithmetic operation can't be performed on a void pointer?

Answer

C language doesn't allow pointer arithmetic on void pointers. The argument being that we don't know the size of what's being pointed to with a void *and therefore can't know how far to seek the pointer to get to the next valid address.

Question #108

What is the use of *fflush*() function?

Answer

The standard input-output functions, like *printf*() and *scanf*(), are buffered, *i.e.*, each device has an associated buffer through which any input or output operation takes place. After an input operation from the standard input device, care should be taken to clear the standard input buffer lest the previous contents of the buffer interfere with subsequent input operations. The function *fflush*() clears the buffer associated with a specified input/output device (*stdin* or *stdout*).

Question #109

Give a method to count the number of ones in a 32 bit number.

Answer

```
int bitcount (unsigned long n)
{
    int count=0;
    while (n) {
        count += n & 0x1u;
        n >> = 1;
    }
    return count;
}
```

Iterated count runs in time proportional to the total number of bits. It simply loops through all the bits, terminating slightly earlier because of the while condition. Useful, if 1's are sparse and among the least significant bits.

Question #110

What is the value of the expression 5["CONQUER"]?

Answer

```
E
```

The string literal "CONQUER" is an array, and the expression is equivalent to "CONQUER"[5]. The inside-out expression is equivalent because *a*[*b*] is equivalent to *(*a*+*b*) which is equivalent to *(*b*+*a*) which is equivalent to *b*[*a*].

Question #111

What is a NULL pointer?

Answer

A NULL pointer is conceptually different from an un-initialized pointer. A NULL pointer is known not to point to any object or function; an un-initialized pointer might point to anywhere. In *stdio.h* header file, NULL is defined as 0. Whenever a program tries to access 0th location, the operating system terminates the program with runtime assignment error because the 0th location is in the operating system's address space and operating system doesn't allow access to its address space by user programs.

Question #112

Predict the output in the following snippet.

```
#include<stdio.h>
int main()
{
   int n[3][3]={ { 1, 2, 3 }, { 4, 5, 6 }, { 7, 8, 9 } };
   printf("%u %u %d", n, n[2], n[2][2]);
}
```

Assume that the array begins at the address 1000.

Answer

```
1000 1024 9
```

Explanation: The 2-D array is stored in memory in continuous locations. There are no rows and columns in memory. A 2-D array is nothing but an array of several 1-D arrays. Here the 1-D array *n*[2] starts at location which is six integers away from the base. Here *n*[2] [2] in the normal indexing into the 2-D array.

❑ ❑ ❑

Chapter 4

Data Structures and Algorithms

Question #1

What is the difference between *data* and *information*?

Answer

Data is just a collection of raw facts and figures from which no conclusions can be drawn. Thus data as such is not useful for decision making. On the other side, information is a processed (refined) form of data. This new generated data (information) conveys some meaning and hence can be used for decision-making.

Question #2

What is a *data structure*? OR Define the term *data structure*.

Answer

Data structure is a logical organization (or mathematical model) of related data in computer's main memory.

Question #3

What is the difference between *data type* and *data structure*?

Answer

Data types are forms of data itself such as Integer, Boolean, String, etc. This is related to how the 1's and 0's are interpreted for that piece of data.

Data structures are arrangements of data items such as arrays, linked lists, stacks, queues, trees, graphs, etc.

Question #4

What are the factors that influence the choice of a particular data structure?

Answer

The following factors influence the choice of a particular data structure:

(*a*) The selected data structure should be capable of representing the relationship that exists among the elements of the data.

(*b*) If more than one data structure is capable of representing the relationship among data elements, then that data structure will be the best choice on which the operations, under consideration, can be implemented more efficiently.

Question #5

What are the areas of study under the domain of the subject of data structures?

OR

What is the scope of the subject of data structures?

Answer

The areas of study (scope) under the domain of the subject of data structures include:

(*a*) Description of the data structures.
(*b*) Representation of the data structures in computer memory.
(*c*) Description of the algorithms implementing various operations on data structures.

Question #6

What are linear data structures?

Answer

Those data structures whose elements form a sequence, e.g., each element is having a unique predecessor except the first element, and each element also has its successor except the last element. Examples are *arrays, linked lists*, *stacks*, and *queues*.

Question #7

What are non-linear data structures?

Answer

Those data structures whose elements don't form a sequence. Examples are *trees* and *graphs.*

Question #8

What is the difference between linear and non-linear data structures?

OR

How non-linear data structures are different from linear data structures?

Answer

In linear data structures, its elements form a sequence whereas in non-linear data structures, their elements don't form a sequence.

Question #9

Which operations are known as dictionary operations?

Answer

The *insert*, *delete* and *search* operations are known as dictionary operations.

Question #10

What is an *algorithm*? What is the criterion that every algorithm must satisfy?

Answer

An *algorithm* is a finite set of steps defining the correct solution of a particular problem.

Each algorithm must satisfy the following criteria:

- **Input** - There are zero or more values which are externally supplied.
- **Output** - At least one value is produced.
- **Definiteness** - Each step must be clear and unambiguous.
- **Finiteness** - If we trace the steps of an algorithm, then for all cases, the algorithm must terminate after a finite number of steps.
- **Effectiveness** - Each step must be sufficiently basic that it can in principle be carried out by a person using only paper and pencil. In addition, not only each step is definite, it must also be feasible.

Question #11

What is *algorithm complexity*? What is the need of measuring the complexity of an algorithm?

Answer

Algorithm complexity basically represents the space and time requirements of an algorithm. It is usually expressed in the form of a function $f(n)$, where n is the input size for a given instance of the problem being solved.

Question #12

What is the need of measuring the complexity of an algorithm?

Answer

There is need to measure complexity of an algorithm because of following reasons:

- To access the resources (memory and CPU time) required by the algorithm to produce the solution of a given problem.
- To compare two or more algorithms for the same problem in order to find which algorithm is more efficient.

Question #13

What are the components of *space complexity*?

Answer

The space needed by a program consists of following components:

- **Instruction space** – space needed to store the executable version of the program and is fixed.

- **Data space** – space needed to store all constants, variable values and has further two components:
    - o Space needed by constants and simple variables. This space is fixed.
    - o Space needed by fixed sized structured variables, such as arrays and structures.
    - o Dynamically allocated space. This space usually varies.
- **Environment stack space** – space needed to store the information needed to resume the suspended (partially completed) functions. Each time a function is invoked, the following data is saved on the environment stack:
    - o Return address, *i.e.*, from where it has to resume after completion of the called function.
    - o Values of all local variables and the values of formal parameters in the function being invoked.

The amount of space needed by recursive functions is called the *recursion stack space*. For each recursive function, this space depends on the space needed by the local variables and the formal parameters. In addition, this space depends on the maximum depth of the recursion, *i.e.*, maximum number of nested recursive calls.

Question #14

What are the components of *time complexity*?

Answer

The time complexity of an algorithm is the amount of time it needs to run to completion. It depends on all factors that the space complexity depends on.

Question #15

What do you mean by *time-space trade-off* among algorithms?

Answer

The best algorithm, hence best program, to solve a given problem is one that requires less space in memory and takes less time to complete its execution. But in practice, it is not always possible to achieve both of these objectives. As said earlier, there may be more than one approach to solve a same problem. One such approach may require more space but takes less time to complete its execution while the other approach requires less space but takes more time to complete its execution. Thus, we may have to sacrifice one at the cost of the other. That is what we can say that there exits a *time-space* trade among algorithms.

Question #16

Which notation is popularly used to express the complexity of an algorithm?

Answer

Big Oh (O) notation is used to express the complexity of an algorithm, for its worst case performance.

Question #17

Describe the *Big Oh* notation.

Answer

Big Oh is a characterization scheme that allows measuring the properties of algorithms such as performance and/or memory requirements in a general fashion. It measures worst case performance, *i.e.*, it gives upper bound.

Suppose, $f(n)$ and $g(n)$ are functions defined on positive integer number n, then function $f(n) = O(g(n))$, read as "*f* of *n* is big oh of *g* of *n*", or as "*f(n)* is of the order of *g(n)*", if there exists positive constants c and n_0, such that $f(n) \leq c \times g(n)$ for all values of $n \geq n_0$.

Question #18

Name the different categories of algorithms based on *Big Oh* notation.

Answer

Based on *Big Oh* notation, algorithms can be categorized as follows:

- Constant time (O(1)) algorithms
- Logarithmic time (O(log$n$)) algorithms
- Linear time (O(n)) algorithms
- Polynomial time (O(n^k), for $k > 1$) algorithms
- Exponential time (O(k^n), for $k > 1$) algorithms

Many algorithms are O($n$log$n$).

Question #19

What are the limitations of *Big Oh* notation?

Answer

Big Oh notation has two basic limitations:

- It contains no consideration of programming effort.
- It masks (hides) potentially important constants.

As an example of later limitation, imagine two algorithms, one using 500000n^2 time, and the other n^3 time. The first algorithm is O(n^2), which implies that it will take less time than the other algorithm which is O(n^3). However, the second algorithm will be faster for $n <$ 500000, and this would be faster for many applications.

Question #20

What is recursion? Which data structure is used to perform recursion?

Answer

Recursion means self-reference, i.e, when a function calls itself directly or indirectly. Code that is capable of being executed in this way is called *re-entrant*.

Many problems are recursive in nature and can be easily solved using recursion, examples include:

- Factorial of a positive number
- Nth Fibonacci number
- Greatest common division (highest common factor)
- Tower of hanoi

Stack is the data structure is used to perform recursion.

Question #21

Which data structure is used to perform recursion?

Answer

Stack is the data structure is used to perform recursion.

Question #22

What is base address?

Answer

It is a starting address of a data structure. Usually used in the context of array.

Question #23

How a linear array is represented in memory?

Answer

A linear array with n elements is represented in computer memory by a contiguous block of requisite memory for the storage of n elements. The computer keeps track of the address of the first element of the array, and the addresses of the other elements are computed at the execution time using the following formulae.

$loc(a[k]) = base(a) + w\,(k - lb)$ in general

$loc(a[k]) = base(a) + w * k$ in C/C++

where w is the number of bytes per storage location for one element in byte organized memory or words per storage locations for one element in the word organized memory.

Question #24

Suppose an array SUM[-20..20] is stored in memory with base address 1000. What will be address of element SUM[-5]? Assume that 2 bytes of memory is required for the storage of each element.

Answer

General formula to compute the address for the above array is

$$loc(a[k]) = base(a) + w\,(k - lb)$$

In our problem, the name of array is *SUM* and value for k is -5, $w = 2$, therefore above formula becomes

$$loc(SUM[-5]) = base(SUM) + 2 \times [\,(-5) - (-20)\,]$$

$$= 1000 + 2 \times [\,-5 + 20\,]$$

$$= 1000 + 2 \times 15 = 1030$$

Question #25

Consider the following statement is C/C++

```
float data[50];
```

If the base address of array *data* is 2000, what will address of the 20th element of the array?

Answer

Formula to compute the address in C/C++ is

$$loc(a[k]) = base(a) + w \times k$$

Since the data type is *float*, and we know that for an element of type float, 4 bytes of memory is required, therefore $w = 4$. We are required to find the address of the 20th element. Note that the index of the 20th element is 19, since the first element is stored at index 0, therefore value for k is 19.

The formula becomes

$$loc(data[19]) = base(data) + 4 \times 19 = 2000 + 4 \times 19 = 2076$$

Question #26

How a two-dimensional (2D) array is represented in memory?

Answer

A 2D array with $m \times n$ elements is represented in computer memory by a contiguous block of requisite memory for the storage of ($m.n$) elements. The computer keeps track of the address of the first element of the array. However, since the computer's memory is a linear memory, the elements of the 2D can be mapped in 1D memory either row-wise or column-wise, and accordingly it said that a 2D array is represented on row-major order or column-major order.

Address of an element in i^{th} row and j^{th} column is computed at the execution time using the following formulae.

Row-major Order

$loc(a[i][j]) = base(a) + w\,[n\,(\,i - lbr\,) + (j - lbc\,)\,]$ in general

$loc(a[i][j]) = base(a) + w\,(\,n \times i\, + j\,)$ in C/C++

Row-major Order

$loc(a[i][j]) = base(a) + w\,[m\,(\,j - lbc\,) + (i - lbr\,)\,]$ in general

$loc(a[i][j]) = base(a) + w\,(\,m \times j\, + i\,)$ in C/C++

where w is the number of bytes per storage location for one element in byte organized memory or words per storage locations for one element in the word organized memory.

Question #27

Suppose an array MAT[-10..10][-10..10] is stored in memory with base address 1000. What will be address of element MAT[-5][2] if the array MAT is stored on row-major order? Assume that 2 bytes of memory is required for the storage of each element.

Answer

Formula for address calculation when a 2D array is stored on row-major order is

$$Loc(MAT[i][j]) = base(MAT) + w\,[n\,(\,i - lbr\,) + (\,j - lbc\,)\,]$$

In our problem, $n = 21$, $w = 2$, $lbc = -10$, $lbr = -10$, therefore, above formula reduces to

$$Loc(MAT[-5][2]) = 1000{+}2{\times}[21{\times}(-5{-}(-10)\,){+}(2{-}(-10)\,)]$$

$$= 1000 + 2 \times [\,21 \times 5 + 12\,]$$

$$= 1000 + 2 \times 117 = 1000 + 234 = 1234$$

Question #28

Suppose an array MAT[-10..10][-10..10] is stored in memory with base address 1000. What will be address of element MAT[-5][2] if the array MAT is stored on column-major order? Assume that 2 bytes of memory is required for the storage of each element.

Answer

Formula for address calculation when a 2D array is stored on column-major order is

$$Loc(MAT[i][j]) = base(MAT) + w\,[m\,(j - lbc) + (i - lbr)]$$

In our problem, $m = 21$, $w = 2$, $lbc = -10$, $lbr = -10$, therefore, above formula reduces to

$$Loc(MAT[-5][2]) = 1000+2\times[21\times(2-(-10))+(-5-(-10))]$$
$$= 1000 + 2 \times [\,21 \times 12 + 5\,]$$
$$= 1000 + 2 \times 257 = 1000 + 514 = 1514$$

Question #29

Consider the following statement is C/C++

```
float mat[20][20];
```

If the base address of array *mat* is 2000, what will address of the element *mat*[5][4]of the array?

Answer

Note that a 2D array is stored on row-major order in C++. Also the lower bound for each index is 0. Since the data type is *float*, and we know that for an element of type float, 4 bytes of memory is required, therefore $w = 4$.

Thus the formula for address calculation

$$loc(a[i][j]) = base(a) + w\,(n \times i + j)$$

becomes

$$loc(mat[5][4]) = base(mat) + 4 \times (20 \times 5 + 4)$$
$$= 2000 + 4 \times (100 + 4) = 2000 + 4 \times 104 = 2416$$

Question #30

What are the limitations of arrays (linear array in particular)?

Answer

The main limitations of linear arrays are

1. The prior knowledge of number of elements in the linear array is necessary.
2. These are static structures. Static in the sense that whether memory is allocated at compilation time or runtime, their memory used by them cannot be reduced or extended.
3. Since the elements of these arrays are stored in consecutive locations, the insertions and deletions in these arrays are time consuming. This is because of moving down or up to creates a space of new element or to occupy the space vacated by the deleted element.

Question #31

What are the aspects in which linear array is a better choice than a linear linked list for implementing a list?

Answer

The only aspects where linear array is a better choice is that if the list is maintained in sorted order, an element can be searched quickly using binary search. On the other hand, a linked list can only by searched sequentially, even if it is sorted.

Question #32

What are the aspects in which linear linked list is a better choice than a linear array for implementing a list?

Answer

The only aspects where linear linked list is a better choice is that additions and deletions can be performed easily and quickly whereas they are very time consuming in case of linear array as, on average, half the elements are moved down and up respectively to accommodate additions and deletions.

Question #33

Differentiate between a linked list and an array.

Answer

Arrays and linked lists are the fundamental data structures. But, these data structures have their own inherit advantages and disadvantages.

The following table gives a comparative view these data structures so that based on the demand of the software under construction, you can take an informative decision to choose array or linked lists to represent your complex data structure.

Table 4.1: Comparative view of arrays and linked lists

Arrays	Linked Lists
Its elements are stored in contiguous memory locations.	Its elements are not stored in contiguous memory locations.
System keeps track of address of the first element only, and the other elements accessed by computing their addresses at execution time using formula for address calculation.	System keeps track of address of the first element only, and the other elements are accessed following the chain of pointers.
It involves no overhead as for memory requirements are concerned.	It involves the overhead of memory for the storage pointers.
Time taken to access any element is same irrespective of its position in the linear array.	Time taken to access an element depends the position of the element in the linear linked list.
Elements can be accessed randomly.	Elements can be accessed in sequence only.
Addition and deletion operations are time consuming since on average half the elements are to moved down or up.	Addition and deletion operations are implemented efficiently by just adjusting few pointers and without disturbing other elements.
If the elements of a linear array are sorted, a given element can be searched quickly using binary search technique.	Even if the elements of a linear linked list are sorted, binary search technique can not be applied as there is no way to compute the address of the middle element.

Question #34

What are various applications of linked lists?

Answer

Like arrays, linked list is a fundamental data structure. It is used in a wide variety of applications. Some of the applications of the linked lists are:

- To build complex data structures such as *stacks*, *queues*, *trees*, and *graphs*.
- To maintain a directory of names.
- To perform arithmetic operations on long integers.
- To manipulate polynomials.
- To represent sparse matrices.

Question #35

How is linear linked list represented in memory?

Answer

In order to represent linear linked list in memory, we will use a record (structure), called *node*, with two fields – first one we will call *info* that will be used to hold information part, and the second we will call *next* that will be used to hold the next pointer field of the node.

In addition, we will also use a *head* variable that holds the address of the first node, *i.e.*, location of the beginning of the list. A special value denoted by *NULL*, will be used to indicate the end of the list, *i.e.*, the *NULL* value in the next pointer field of a node will indicate that it is the last node of the list.

To start with, pointer variable *head* is assigned NULL value to indicate that linear linked list is initially empty.

In C language the required declarations would look like

```
typedef struct nodeType
{
   int info;
   struct nodeType *next;
} node;

node *head = NULL;
```

Question #36

How is doubly linked list represented in memory?

Answer

In order to represent doubly linked list in memory, we will use a record (structure), called *node*, with three fields – first one we will call *info* that will be used to hold information part, the second we will call *next* that will be used to hold the next pointer field of the node, and the third *prev* that will used to hold the previous pointer field of the node.

In addition, we will also use *head* variable that holds the address of the first node, *i.e.*, location of the beginning of the list, and *tail* variable that holds the address of the last node, *i.e.*, location of the end of the list. A special value denoted by *NULL*, when used in the *next* pointer field indicates that there is no node after this node, and when used in the *prev* pointer field indicates that there is no node preceding this node.

To start with both pointers variables, *head* and *tail*, are assigned NULL value to indicate that doubly linked list is initially empty.

In C language the required declarations would look like

```
typedef struct nodeType
{
    struct nodeType *prev;
    int info;
    struct nodeType *next;
} node;

node *head = NULL, *tail = NULL;
```

Question #37

What is last-in-first-out (LIFO)?

Answer

It is a method of linear management in which the element most recently added to the list would be the next element taken out of the list; defines the mode of operation of a stack.

Question #38

How a stack can be represented using linear array?

Answer

To represent a stack we need a variable, called *top*, that holds the index of the top element of the stack and an array to hold the elements of the stack. Let us suppose that the elements of the stack are of integer type, and the stack can store maximum of 10 such elements, *i.e.*, stack size is 10.

The following are the necessary declarations in C language

```
#define  MAX  10
typedef struct
{
   int top;
   int elements[MAX];
} STACK;
STACK stk;
```

We have defined our own data type named *stack*, which is structure and whose first element *top* will be used as an index to the top element, and an array *elements* of size MAX whose elements are of integer type, to hold the elements of the stack. The last line declares variable *stk* of type *STACK*.

Question #39

How a stack can be represented using linear linked list?

Answer

To represent a stack using linear linked list, the *info* field of the node hold the elements of the stack while the *next* field hold the pointers to the neighbouring elements of the stack. The pointer variable *top* (instead of *start/head* consistent with the stack terminology) is used to hold the address (pointer) of the first (top most) element.

Note that the first element of the linear linked list is the element at the top of the stack and the last element of the linear linked list is the element at the bottom of the stack.

Therefore, the push operation is implemented by inserting new element at the beginning of the list, and the pop operation is implemented by removing the element from the beginning of the list.

The following are the necessary declarations in C language

```
typedef struct nodeType {
    int info;
    struct nodeType *next;
 } STACK;

STACK *top;
```

We have defined our own data type named *STACK,* which is a self-referential structure and whose first element *info* hold the element of the stack and the second element *next* holds the address of the element under it in the stack. The last line declares a pointer variable *top* of type *STACKS.*

Question #40

Given a choice, which fundamental data structure – *linear array* or *linear linked list*, you will use to represent a stack in memory and why?

Answer

Linear linked list, because stack when represented using linear array suffers from following problems:

- Size of the stack must be known in advance.
- We may come across situations when an attempt to push an element causes overflow. However, stack, as an abstract data structure can not be full. Hence, abstractly, it is always possible to push an element onto stack. Therefore, representing stack as an array prohibits the growth of stack beyond the finite number of elements.

The linked list representation allows a stack to grow to a limit of the computer's memory.

Question #41

What are various operations that can be performed on a stack named *S*?

Answer

The following operations are performed on stacks.

1. CreateStack(*S*) – to create *S* as an empty stack.
2. Push(*S, item*) – to push element *item* onto stack *S*.
3. Pop(*S, item*) – to remove the top element of the stack *S*.
4. Peep(*S, item*) – to access the top element of the stack *S* without removing it from the stack *S*.
5. IsFull(*S, status*) – to check whether the stack *S* is full.
6. IsEmpty(*S, status*) – to check whether the stack *S* is empty.

Question #42

What is the complexity of various operations that can be performed on a stack?

Answer

The complexity of all the operations is O(1), i.e., independent of the size of the stack (number of elements in the stack).

Irrespective of the number of elements in the stack, the time taken by each operation is same as same instruction are executed.

Question #43

What is the difference between *pop()* and *peep()* operations?

Answer

The *pop()* operation removes and returns the top element of the stack where as the *peep()* operation simply returns the top element of the stack, it does not remove the top element from the stack.

Question #44

What are application areas of stacks?

Answer

Stack is one of the important data structure. It finds application in many areas, some of them include

- Arithmetic evaluations.
- Implementing recursive solution.
- Handling function calls.

- Handling local variables in functions.
- Heavily used by the system itself for housekeeping job.
- Used in housekeeping for solving many other problems such as traversals of trees and graphs.

Question #45

Show how the stack is used to convert the following infix expression *q*:

(7 – 5) * (9 / 2)

to postfix notation.

Answer

Progress of the algorithm to translate *q* to postfix expression *p* is shown in Table 4.2.

Table 4.2: Conversion from Infix to Postfix Notation

Character Scanned	Stack	Expression *p*
(	(	
7	(	7
–	(, –	7
5	(, –	7, 5
)	Empty	7, 5, –
*	*	7, 5, –
(	*, (	7, 5, –
9	*, (	7, 5, –, 9
/	*, (, /	7, 5, –, 9
2	*, (, /	7, 5, –, 9, 2
)	*	7, 5, –, 9, 2, /
End of expression	Empty	7, 5, –, 9, 2, /, *

Question #46

Show how the stack is used to solve the following arithmetic expression *p* given in postfix notation:

7, 5, –, 9, 2, /, *

to postfix notation.

Answer

Progress of algorithm to evaluate postfix expression *p* is shown in Table 4.3.

Table 4.3: Evaluation of Postfix Expression

Character Scanned	Stack
7	7
5	7, 5
–	2
9	2, 9
2	2, 9, 2
/	2, 4.5
*	9
End of expression	9

The final number in stack, *i.e.*, 9, is the value of postfix expression *p*.

Question #47

What is last-in-first-out (FIFO) or last-come-first-serve (FCFS)?

Answer

It is a method of linear management in which the elements are taken out in the order in which they are added to the list; defines the mode of operation of a queue.

Question #48

What are various operations that can be performed on a stack named *S*?

Answer

The following operations, for full functionality, are performed on queue *Q*:

1. CreateQueue(*Q*) – to create *q* as an empty queue.
2. Enque(*Q*, *item*) – to insert (add) element *item* in a queue *q*.
3. Dequeue(*Q*) – to remove element of queue *q*.

4. Peep(*Q*) – to access the first element of the queue *q* without removing it.
5. IsFull(*Q*) – to check whether the queue *q* is full.
6. IsEmpty(*Q*) – to check whether the queue *q* is empty.

Question #49

What is the complexity of various operations that can be performed on a queue?

Answer

The complexity of all the operations is O(1), i.e., independent of the size of the queue (number of elements in the queue).

Question #50

How a queue is represented in memory using an array?

Answer

A queue is represented by a linear array, say *queue*, and two integer variables *front* and *rear*. Here variable *front* holds the index of the first element of the queue, and variable *rear* holds the index of the last element of the queue.

Question #51

What is a priority queue?

Answer

A *priorities queue* is a kind of queue in which each element is assigned a priority and the order in which elements are deleted and processed comes from the following rules:

- Element with highest priority is processed first before any element of lower priority.
- Two or more elements with the same priority are processed according to the order in which they were added to the queue.

Question #52

What are different criteria's for determining the priority?

Answer

There different criteria's for determining the priority include:

- A shortest job is given higher priority over the longer one.
- An important job is given higher priority over a routine type job. For example, a transaction for on-line booking of an order is given preference over payroll processing.
- In a commercial computer center, the amount you pay for the job can determine priority for your job. Pay more to get higher priority for your job.

Question #53

How a priority queue can be represented in memory?

Answer

A priority queue can be represented in memory using:

- *Linear linked list* — In this representation, each node of the linked list will have three fields:
  - An information field *info* that hold the element of the queue,
  - A priority filed *prn* that holds the priority number of the element, and
  - A next pointer filed *link* that holds pointer to next element of the queue.

  Further, a node *X* precedes a node *Y* in the linear linked list if either node *X* has higher priority that *Y* or both nodes have same priority but *X* was added to the list before *Y*.
- *Multiple queues, one for each priority* — In this representation, one queue is maintained for each priority number. In order to process an element of the priority queue, element from the first non-empty highest priority number queue is accessed. In order to add a new element to the priority queue, the element is inserted in an appropriate queue for given priority number.

- *Heap* — A priority queue having highest priority for lower number can be represented using *min heap*, and a priority queue having highest priority for higher number can be represented using *max heap*.

  The element of the priority queue to be processed next is always in the root node of the heap.

Question #54

What is a deque?

Answer

A *deque*, pronounced as *deck*, a kind of linear queue in which elements can be added/removed at/from either end but not in the middle. The term deque is a contraction of the name *double-ended queue*.

Question #55

What are variations of a deque?

Answer

There are two variations of a deque, which are intermediate between a deque and a queue. These are:

- *Input-restricted deque* – which allows insertions only at one end but allows deletions at both ends.
- *Output-restricted deque* – which allows insertions at both ends but allows deletions only at one end.

Question #56

What is a rooted tree?

Answer

It is a tree in which one node, called the *root*, is distinguished from other nodes.

Question #57

What is a height balanced tree?

Answer

It is a binary tree where for each node *R*, the height of the left subtree of *R* and height of the right subtree *R* differ by at most 1.

Question #58

What is meant by degree of an element?

Answer

The degree of a tree is the maximum of its element degrees.

Question #59

What is the height of a tree?

Answer

If level of the root is denoted by 1, then the maximum level number of the tree is known as its *height*.

Question #60

What is the weight of a tree?

Answer

It is the number of leaf nodes in a tree.

Question #61

What do similar trees mean?

Answer

Trees that have the same structure and but different node contents. For example:

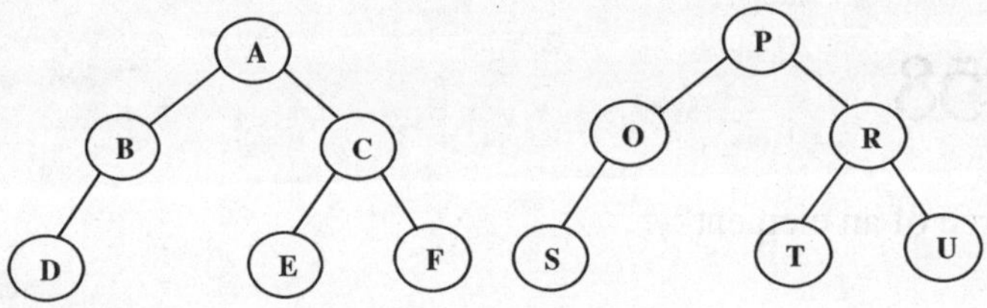

Question #62

What do equivalent trees mean?

Answer

Trees that have the same structure and node contents. For example:

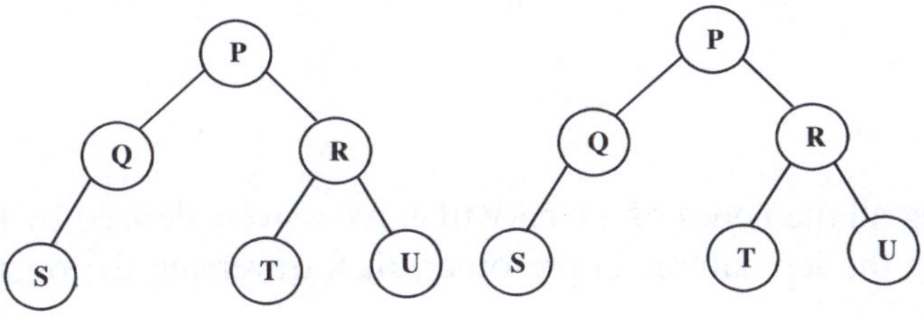

Question #63

What is an in-order traversal?

Answer

It is a method of visiting all the nodes of a binary tree, recursively defined by first traversing the left subtree in in-order, then visiting the root, then traversing the right subtree in in-order.

Question #64

What is a post-order traversal?

Answer

It is a method of visiting all the nodes of a binary tree, recursively defined by first traversing the left subtree in post-order, then traversing the right subtree in post-order, then visiting the root.

Question #65

What is a pre-order traversal?

Answer

It is a method of visiting all the nodes of a binary tree, recursively defined by first visiting the root, then traversing the left subtree in pre-order, then traversing the right subtree in pre-order.

Question #66

A binary search tree provides best of both of arrays and linked lists. How?

Answer

Note that a binary search tree is represented using linked list. Since the elements in a binary search tree are ordered, so search operation can be implemented efficiently. Since linked list is to represent a binary search tree, the new element can be added or exiting element can be deleted quickly.

Question #67

If there are n elements ($n > 0$), what will be the number of edges?

Answer

Every element in a binary tree, except the root, has exactly one parent. There is exactly one edge between each child and its parent. So the number of edges is $n-1$.

Question #68

What can be the minimum and maximum number of elements in a binary tree of height h, $h > 0$?

Answer

Since there must be at least one element at each level, the number of elements is at least h. As each element can have at most two children, the number of elements at level k is at most 2^{k-1} for $k > 0$. For $h = 0$, the total number of elements is 0, which equals 2^0-1. For $h > 0$, the total number of elements cannot exceed $\sum_{k=1}^{h} 2^{k-1} = 2^h - 1$.

Question #69

What can be the minimum and maximum height of a binary tree that contains n elements ($n > 0$)?

Answer

Since there must be at least one element at each level, the height cannot exceed n. We also know that a binary tree of height h can have no more than 2^h-1 elements.

Therefore, $n \le 2^h-1$. Hence $h \ge \log_2(n+1)$. Further, since h is an integer, we get $h \ge \lceil \log_2(n+1) \rceil$.

Question #70

What is a full binary tree?

Answer

A binary tree of height h that contains exactly 2^h-1 elements is called a *full binary tree*.

Question #71

What is a complete binary tree?

Answer

Binary tree is said to be *complete* if all its levels, except the last, have maximum number of possible nodes, and if all the nodes at the last level appear as far as left as possible, *i.e.*, if at the second last level, a node have only one child it will be the left one.

Question #72

What is an extended binary tree or 2 tree?

Answer

A binary tree is said to be a *2-tree* or an *extended binary tree* if each node has either 0 or 2 children. In such a case, the nodes with 2 children are called *internal nodes*, the nodes with 0 children are called *external nodes*. Usually the nodes are distinguished in diagram by using circles for internal nodes and squares for external nodes.

Question #73

How a binary tree can be represented in computer memory?

Answer

A binary three can be represented in memory using a linear array or a linked list with two pointer fields.

In case of linear array, the relationship of node with its left and right child is represented as follows — for each node at indexes *i*, if it has a left child it will be at index 2*i* and if it also has a right child it will be at index 2*i*+1.

In case of linked list, the relationship of node with its left and right child is represented as follows — for each node, if it has a left child its address will be in the left pointer field and if it also has a right child its address will be in the right pointer fields. The non-presence of a child is indicated by the sentinel value NULL (×) in the appropriate pointer field.

Consider the following binary tree

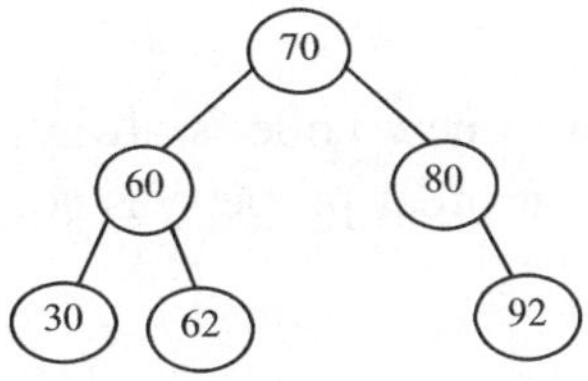

Using linear array, it will be represented as

1	2	3	4	5	6	7	8	9	10
70	60	80	30	62		92			

And using linked list, it will be represented as

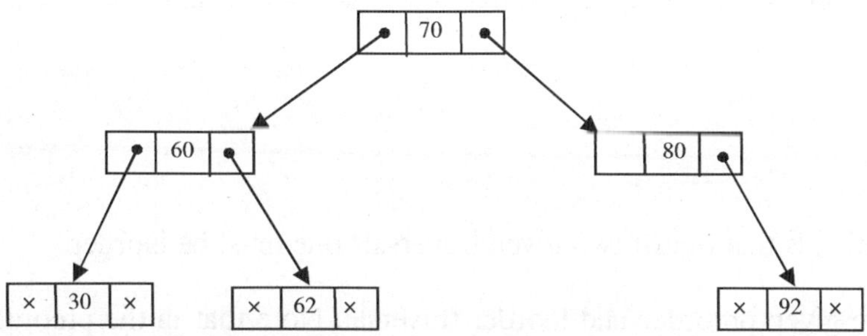

The declarations, in C, for linked list representation will look like

```
struct nodeType
{
   struct nodeType *left;
   int info;
   struct nodeType *right;
} NODE;
```

Question #74

Whether newly inserted node in a binary search tree becomes internal or external node?

Answer

New node inserted is always inserted as external node. Note that a new node is always inserted as a external node, as a child of an appropriate node so that order property is not disturbed.

Question #75

Is it possible to construct a binary search tree if at least two traversal of a binary search tree are given?

Answer

Yes. The condition is that out of two given traversals one must be inorder.

Suppose we are given preorder and inorder traversal. Note that in the preorder traversal, the first element is the root of the binary search tree. Now locate this element in the inorder and the elements to its left are elements of left subtree of the root node and elements to its right are elements of the right subtree. Again the repeat the same steps for each of the sub trees.

In case we are given postorder and inorder traversal. Note that in the postorder traversal, the last element is the root of the binary search tree. Now locate this element in the inorder and the elements to its left are elements of left subtree of the root node and elements to its right are elements of the right subtree. Again the repeat the same steps for each of the sub trees.

Question #76

What do you mean by (inorder) successor and (inorder) predecessor of a given node in a binary search tree?

Answer

Note that the inorder traversal lists the nodes in the ascending order. The node preceeding to a given node in this listing is called predecessor of the node and node following it is called its successor.

Question #77

Deleting a node form the binary search tree is the most difficult operations among various operations performed on a binary search tree. How it is accomplished?

Answer

For deleting a node, following cases may arise:

Case 1: Node *N* has no children, then node *N* is deleted from binary search tree by replacing the location of node *N* in the parent node by the NULL pointer.

Case 2: Node *N* has only one child, then node *N* is deleted from binary search tree by replacing the location of node *N* in the parent node by the only child of node *N*, and then deleting the child (case 1).

Case 3: Node *N* has two children, then node *N* is deleted form the binary search tree by replacing it either by its predecessor (or successor), then deleting the predecessor (or successor). Note that the predecessor or successor is either a terminal node or node with one child, *i.e.*, the case of deleting a predecessor or successor reduces to deleting a node with no child (case 1) or deleting a node with only one child (case 2).

Question #78

How can we find the mirror image of a binary tree?

Answer

A mirror image of a binary tree can be obtained by interchanging the left child with the right child at every node. This task can be best implemented using recursion — if binary tree is not empty then first we find the mirror image of the left subtree and then mirror image of the right subtree, and finally we interchange the left subtree with right subtree. The following function shows the actual details:

```
void MirrorImage( NODE *tree )
{
   NODE *temp;
   if ( tree != NULL ) {
      MirrorImage( tree->left );
      MirrorImage( tree->right );
      temp = tree->left;
      tree->left = tree->right;
      tree->right = temp;
   }
}
```

Question #79

What is an AVL tree?

Answer

A binary search tree T with T_L and T_R as its left and right sub tree, then T is an AVL tree if and only if

1. $|h_L - h_R| \leq 1$, where h_L and h_R are the heights of T_L and T_R, respectively, and
2. T_L and T_R are AVL trees.

The height of an empty (null) AVL tree is taken as −1.

Question #80

How an AVL tree is represented in memory?

Answer

The node in an *AVL* tree will have an additional field *bf* (for balance factor) in addition to the structure of a node in a binary search tree.

The value for field *bf* is chosen as

$$bf = \begin{cases} -1 & if\ \ h_L < h_R \\ 0 & if\ \ h_L = h_R \\ +1 & if\ \ h_L > h_R \end{cases}$$

Examples:

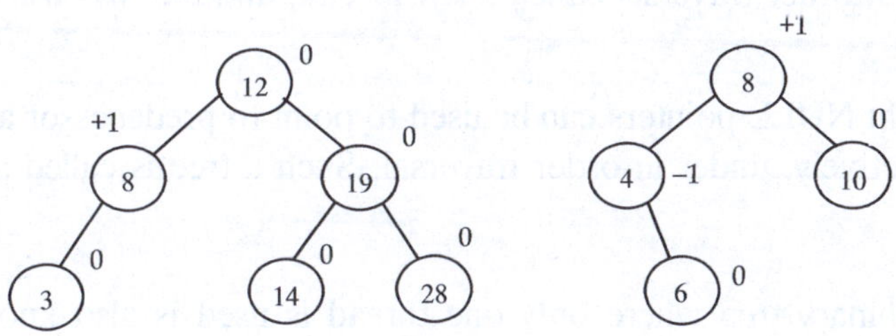

Each node is labeled with the balance factor (*bf*).

Question #81

What is rotation, in the context of trees?

Answer

It is a type of restructuring applied to a tree to return it to a state of balance.

Question #82

What is a threaded tree?

Answer

It is a tree that uses its unused pointers in a node to point to its predecessor and/or successor in an inorder traversal.

There are many ways to thread a binary tree. These are

- The right NULL pointer of each node can be replaced by a thread to the successor of that node under in-order traversal called a *right thread*, and the tree will be called a *right-threaded tree*.
- The left NULL pointer of each node can be replaced by a thread to the predecessor of that node under in-order traversal called a *left thread*, and the tree will be called a *left-threaded tree*.
- Both left and right NULL pointers can be used to point to predecessor and successor of that node, respectively, under in-order traversal. Such a tree is called a *fully threaded tree*.

Note: A threaded binary tree where only one thread is used is also known as *one-way threaded tree* and where both the threads are used is also known as *two-way threaded tree*.

Question #83

What is a max heap?

Answer

It is an almost complete binary tree, in which the key values are arranged such that for each node i, $key(i) \leq key(j)$, where j is the father of node i.

Question #84

What is an *m*-way search tree?

Answer

It is a tree in which each node has out-degree ≤ *m*, each node is composed of a set of pointers and key values, and the key values are arranged in a specific manner that facilitates search through the pointer structures. Examples are B, B^+, B^* trees. Note that binary search tree is a 2-way search tree.

Question #85

What is a B-tree?

Answer

A *B-tree of order m* is an *m*-way search tree with the following properties:

- Each node of the tree, except the root node and leaves, has at least *m*/2 sub trees and no more than *m* sub trees.
- Root of the tree has at least two sub trees unless it is a leaf node.
- All leaves of the tree are on the same level.

Question #86

What is a B^+-tree?

Answer

It is a B-tree in which the leave nodes are linked to each other from left to right to form a linked list of the keys in sequential order.

Question #87

What is a B^*-tree?

Answer

It is a B-tree in which each interior node is at least two-third full rather than just half full.

Question #88

What is simple graph?

Answer

It is a graph that has no loops and in which no pair of nodes is connected by more than one edge.

Question #89

What is a connected graph?

Answer

A graph *G* is said to be *connected* if there is path between any two of its vertices, *i.e.*, there is no isolated vertex.

A connected graph without any cycles is called a *tree*. Thus we can say that tree is a special graph.

Question #90

What is a complete graph?

Answer

A graph G is said to *complete* or *fully connected* if there is path from every vertex to every other vertex. A complete graph with n vertices will have $n(n\text{-}1)/2$ edges.

Question #91

What is an activity graph?

Answer

It is a graph representing the precedence required and parallelism possible among set of activities or task where the nodes represent the activities and the edges represent precedence requirements.

Question #92

What is the difference between a *tree* and a *graph*?

Answer

The only difference is that a tree cannot have a cycle. Thus, every tree is a graph but only graph without a cycle qualifies to be tree.

Question #93

What is a directed acyclic graph (DAG)?

Answer

A directed acyclic graph (DAG) G is a directed graph without cycle(s).

Question #94

What is a strongly connected graph?

Answer

A directed graph G is said to be *strongly connected*, if for each pair u, v of vertices in G, if there exists a path from u to v, there must exist a path from v to u; otherwise the directed graph is *unilaterally connected.*

Question #95

If there are ten edges in an undirected graph, what will be the number of nodes in adjacency lists?

Answer

Number of nodes will be 20, since for an edge $[i, j]$, vertex j will exist in the adjacency list for vertex i, and vertex i will exist in the adjacency list for vertex j.

Question #96

Compare and contrast between BFS and DFS.

Answer

The BFS systematically explores the edges of G breadth wise from the source vertex s. It first traverses the vertices adjacent to the root, then their adjacent vertices and so on.

The DFS, as its name implies, is to traverse *deeper* in the graph, whenever possible. The edges are explored out of the most recently discovered vertex v that still has unexplored edges leaving it. When all of v's edges have been explored, the search *backtracks* to explore edges leaving the vertex from which v was discovered. This process continues until we have discovered all the vertices that are reachable from the source vertex s.

Question #97

What is a topological sort?

Answer

A *topological sort* of a directed acyclic graph (DAG) $G = (V, E)$ is a linear ordering of all its vertices such that if G contains an edge (u, v), then u appears before v in the ordering.

A topological sort of a graph can be viewed as an ordering of its vertices along a horizontal line so that all directed edges go from left to right.

Question #98

What is a minimum spanning tree?

Answer

It is a spanning tree that has a minimum cost among all spanning trees. It may happen that more than one spanning tree has a minimum cost.

Question #99

What is an articulation point in a graph?

Answer

Let $G = (V, E)$ be a connected, undirected graph. An *articulation point*, also called a *cut point*, of G is a vertex whose removal disconnects G.

Question #100

What is a bridge in a graph?

Answer

Let $G = (V, E)$ be a connected, undirected graph. A *bridge* of G is an edge whose removal disconnects G.

Question #101

What is an Eulerian tour?

Answer

An *Eulerian tour* through an undirected graph is a path whose edge list contains each edge of the graph exactly once.

An *Eulerian graph* is a graph that possesses an Eulerian tour.

Question #102

What is a Hamiltonian tour?

Answer

A *Hamiltonian tour* through an undirected graph is a path whose vertex list contains each vertex of the graph exactly once.

A *Hamiltonian graph* is a graph that possesses a Hamiltonian tour.

Question #103

Which data structure efficiently supports dictionary operations?

Answer

Hash table is the best data structure that efficiently supports dictionary operations.

Question #104

What is a hash table?

Answer

A *hash table*, in basic sense, is a generalization of the simpler notion of a linear array, whose size is of the order of the active keys. Further, instead of using the key as array index directly, the array index is computed from the key by manipulating it using some mathematical function, called *hash function*.

Question #105

What is hashing?

Answer

It is an address calculation technique. While in a direct-address table, an element with key k is stored in slot k, whereas this element is stored in a hash table at slot $h(k)$; that is, a *hash function h* is used to compute the slot from the key k. Here, the *hash function h* maps the universe U of keys into the slots of a hash table, say $T[0..m-1]$. This process of mapping keys to appropriate slots in a hash table is known as *hashing*.

Question #106

What is a hash function?

Answer

A hash function h is simply a mathematical formula that manipulates the key in some form to compute the index for this key in the hash table. In general, we say that a hash function h maps the universe U of keys into the slots of a hash table $T[0..m-1]$.

Question #107

What is a collision?

Answer

Collision is a situation, when more than one key maps to the same index in a hash table.

Question #108

What are the techniques/schemes to resolve collisions?

Answer

Following techniques/schemes are used for resolving collisions:

- By separating chaining.
- By open addressing.

Question #109

What should be the main considerations while choosing a particular hash function?

Answer

The main considerations while choosing a particular hash function include

- It should be easy to compute.
- It should distribute the keys uniformly across the hash-table, *i.e.*, it should keep the number of collisions as minimum as possible.

Question #110

What are various hash functions?

Answer

Few popular hash functions are

- Division method
- Multiplication method
- Midsquare method
- Folding method

Question #112

How collisions are resolved using separate chaining?

Answer

The collision resolution by separating chaining, also called *synonyms chaining*. In this scheme, all the elements whose keys hash to the same hash-table index are put in a one linked list .

Question #113

How collisions are resolved using open addressing?

Answer

In the open addressing scheme all the elements are stored in the hash-table itself. In order to insert a key in a hash table under this scheme, if the slot to which key is hashed is free then the element is stored at that slot. In case the slot is filled, then other slots are examined systematically, in the forward direction, to find the free slot. If no such slot is found then overflow condition occurs.

Question #114

What is rehashing?

Answer

If at any stage the hash table becomes nearly full, the running time for the operations will start taking too much time. This can happen if there are too many deletions intermixed with too many insertions.

In such a situation, the best possible solution is to rehash the keys by performing following steps:

1. Create a new hash table of size double than the original hash table.
2. Scan the original hash table, and for each key, compute the new hash value and insert into the new hash table.
3. Free the memory occupied by the original hash table.

Question #115

What is binary search? What is its complexity?

Answer

A search technique that is applied to a list of ordered keys. At each step of the search, the list is partitioned into two equal parts, with the selection of the appropriate partition to probe in the next iteration made on the basis of relative key values. Its complexity is $O(n\log_2 n)$.

Question #116

Can we apply binary search on a sorted linear linked list?

Answer

No. Because there is no way to compute the address of the middle element as the elements of the linear linked list are not stored in contagious memory locations.

Question #117

Name the conditions under which sequential (linear) search of the list is preferable over the binary search.

Answer

Possible conditions can be

- List is not sorted.
- We want to find all the occurrences of a given element.
- List is stored in memory using a linked list.

Question #118

What is an internal sort?

Answer

It is a method for arranging a collection of key values into a specified order, where the collection resides in main memory.

Question #119

What is an external sort?

Answer

A method for arranging a collection of key values into a specified order, where the collection resides on a secondary storage device. Read/write time is a significant factor in determining sort performance. Also called a *file sort*.

Question #120

What is an exchange sort?

Answer

It is a family of internal sort algorithms in which pairs of key values are compared and exchanged if they are not in proper relative positions.

Question #121

What is partition-exchange Sort?

Answer

It is an exchange sort where at each step of the sort, the list is partitioned into two parts such that the key values in one partition are less than a particular key value and key values in the other partition are greater than particular key value. Further, these partitions are then treated independently in following steps of the sort. Example is quicksort.

Question #122

What is a quicksort?

Answer

It is an internal sort where at each step of the sort, the list is partitioned into two parts such that the key values in one partition are less than a particular key value and key values in the other partition are greater than particular key value. Further, these partitions are then treated independently in following steps of the sort.

Question #123

What is best case and worst case complexity of quicksort? Explain

Answer

Best case complexity: $O(n\log_2 n)$
Worst case complexity: $O(n^2)$

Question #124

What are the similarities and difference between merge sort and quick sort algorithms?

Answer

Similarities:

- Both are based on divide-and-conquer technique.
- Both give worst case complexity of $O(n\log_2 n)$.

Differences:

- Merge sort works bottom-up while quick sort works top-down.
- Merge sort the elements by merging while quick sort works by partitioning.
- Best case as well as worst case complexity of Merge sort is $O(n\log_2 n)$ where as best case complexity is $O(n\log_2 n)$ and worst case complexity is $O(n^2)$ in case of Quick sort.
- Memory requirements of merge sort are double as that of quick sort because merge sort uses a local array of the same size as that of given array for merging the sorted sub arrays.

❑ ❑ ❑

Chapter 5

Object-Oriented Concepts

Question #1

What is procedural (structured) programming?

Answer

In *procedural programming*, also known by other names as *structured programming*, *functional programming* or *traditional programming*, the problem in hand is viewed as a sequence of things to be done such as reading, calculating and printing. Separate functions are written to accomplish these tasks. Thus, the primary focus is on functions.

In other words, we can say that a given problem is divided into small sized sub problems; each sub problem represents a specific task that can be handled efficiently and effectively. Then to solve each sub problem, a function is written.

The technique of hierarchical decomposition has been used to specify the tasks to be completed to find the solution of a problem.

Note here that there is no mention of data. These functions are written to manipulate the data to accomplish a specific task. Thus, the data that is key to the existence of functions and hence a program gets a raw treatment.

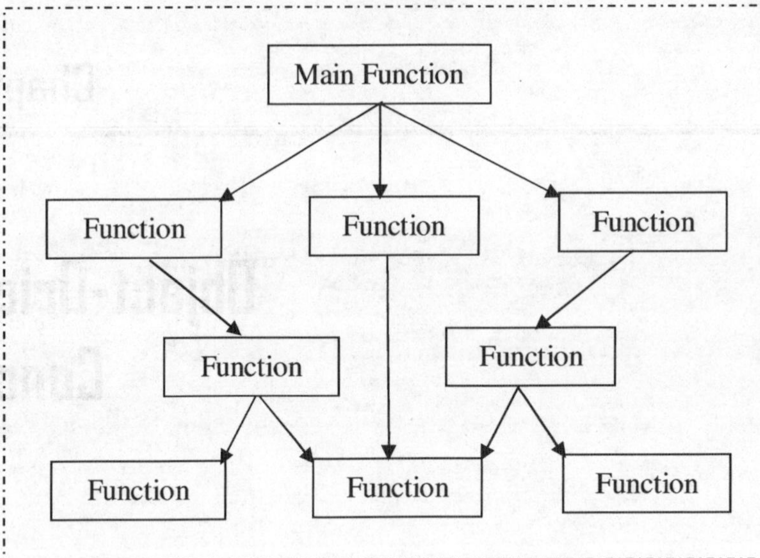

Figure 5.1: Typical structure of a procedural program

Further, the data in a procedural program is spread across entire software in the form of local and global data structures. The global data is more vulnerable to an inadvertent change by a function. Functions communicate with each other either by passing arguments or by accessing and modifying data structures. In a very large program it is very difficult to identify what data is used by which function.

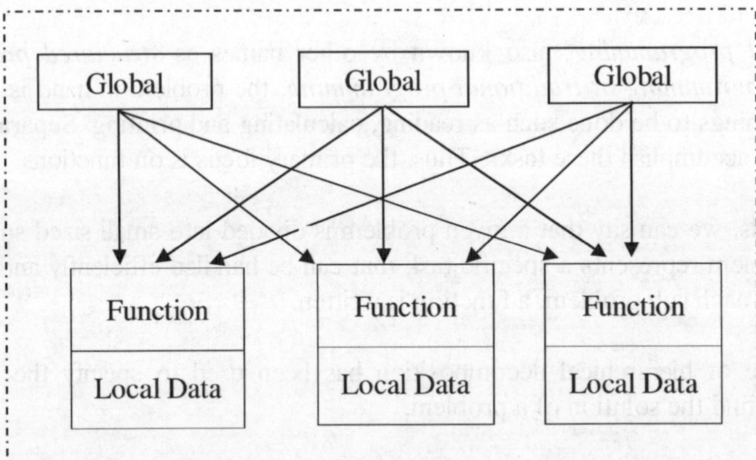

Figure 5.2: Relationship of data and functions in a procedural program

Question #2

What are the key characteristics of procedural (structured) programming?

Answer

Key characteristics of procedural (structured) programming are

- Emphasis is on doing things (algorithms).
- Large programs are divided into smaller independent subprograms known as functions or procedures (algorithmic decomposition).
- Majority the functions share global data.
- Data is scattered around the program in the form of local and shared data.
- Functions transform data from one form to another.
- Employs *top-down* approach to program design.

Question #3

What are the disadvantages/limitations of procedural programming?

Answer

- The procedural programming approach does not model the real world problems very well.
- The program logic is dependent on the organisation of the data and the vice a versa. You cannot change one without change to another.
- The parts of the program are heavily dependent on each other, *i.e.*, tightly coupled to each other. Therefore, it is very difficult to make a change in one part of the program without affecting the other part.

These problems magnify further as the size and the complexity of the problem under consideration increases, and almost become unmanageable for very large and complex systems.

Question #4

What is object-oriented programming?

Answer

The major motivation for the invention of new programming approach, object-oriented programming, was to remove the flaws of procedural programming approach. Object-oriented programming treats the data as a most critical element in the program design and does not allow it be scattered around the program. It ties the data and the functions that operate on it and protects it from the other functions.

Object-oriented programming allows decomposition of a problem into a number of entities called *objects* and then builds data and functions around these objects.

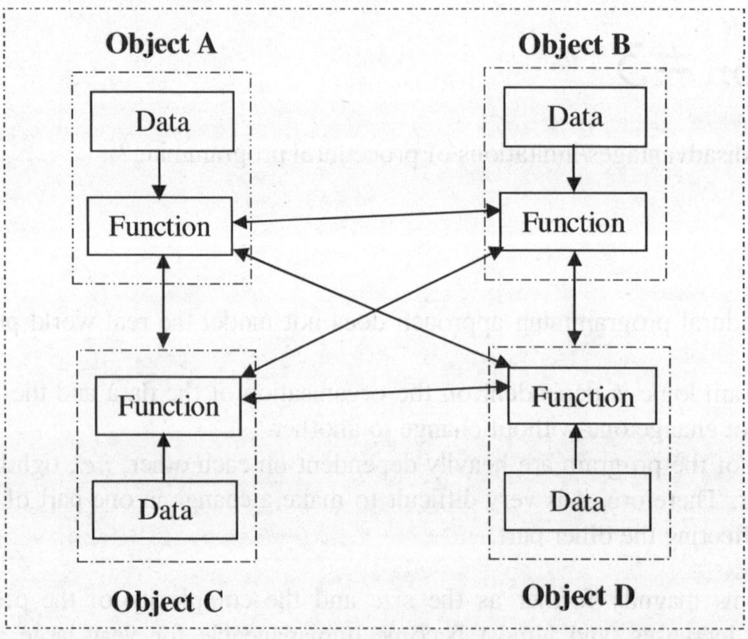

Figure 5.3: Typical Structure of an object-oriented program

The data of an object can only be accessed by functions associated with it. However, function of one object can access the function of another object. The communications among functions of different objects is called *messaging*.

Question #5

What are key characteristics of object-oriented programming?

Answer

Key characteristics of object-oriented programming are:

- Emphasis is on data rather than functions.
- Programs are divided into set of related objects.
- Data structures are designed in such way so as to characterize the objects.
- Functions that operate on the data of an object are tied together with the data structure.
- Data of an object is hidden and cannot be accessed by external functions.
- Objects communicate with each other through functions.
- Employs *bottom-up* approach to program design.

The organization of programs using object-oriented programming approach overcomes all the problems of procedural programming.

Question #6

What is an object model?

Answer

Object model is a description of an object-oriented architecture, including the details of the object structure, interfaces between objects and other object-oriented features and functions.

It encompasses the principles of *abstraction*, *encapsulation*, *data hiding*, *inheritance*, *overloading*, and *polymorphism*.

Nothing is new about these principles. The important feature of the object model is that these elements are brought together in a synergistic way.

Question #7

How formally can we define object-oriented programming?

Answer

The object-oriented programming can formally be defined as *a method of implementation in which programs are organized as cooperative collection of objects, each of which represent an instance of some class, and whose classes are all members of a hierarchy of classes united via inheritance relationship*.

The object-oriented programming use objects as basic building blocks, where each object is an instance of some class, and classes are related to each other through inheritance.

Question #8

List various concepts and terms that are used extensively in object-oriented programming.

Answer

Extensively used concepts and terms in object-oriented programming include:

- Object
- Class
- Abstraction
- Encapsulation
- Data Hiding
- Inheritance
- Overloading
- Polymorphism
- Dynamic binding
- Message passing

Question #9

Differentiate between a class and an object?

Answer

The concepts of class and object are tightly interwoven, for example, we cannot talk about an object without regard for its class.

However, there are important differences between these two terms. An object is a concrete entity that exists in time and space. A class represents only an abstraction, the *essence* of an object, as it were. Thus, we may speak of the class mammal, which represents characteristics common to all mammals. To identify a particular mammal in this class, we must speak of *this mammal* or *that mammal*.

In the context of object-oriented programming, we define class as a set of objects that share a common structure and a common behaviour. A single object is simply an instance of a class.

Question #10

What is an object?

Answer

An *object* is an entity that has *state*, *behavior* and *identity*. The structure and behavior of similar objects are defined in their common class. The term *instance* and *object* are interchangeable.

Question #11

Give some examples of classes and objects from the real-world and programming world?

Answer

Examples from real-world:

Class	Objects
Bird	Sparrow, Parrot, Peacock, etc.
Car	Santro, Swift, Punto, etc.
Mammal	Cow, Buffalo, Goat, etc.
Human Being	Meahk, Pradeep, Shalini, etc.

Examples from programming-world:

Class	Objects
Complex Number	2.5+7.5*i*, 3.0 -5.5*i*, etc.
Shape	Cricle, Line, Rectangle, etc.
GUI Element	Menu, Toolbar, Button, etc.
Linked List	L1, L2, L3, etc.

Question #12

What are the characteristics of an object?

Answer

Each object has following characteristics:

- *State* – The *state* of an object encompasses all of the (usually static) property of the object plus the current (usually dynamic) values of each of these properties.
- *Behavior* – The *behavior* of an object tells how it acts and reacts to the outside world in terms of its state changes and message passing.

  With this, the state of the object can now be defined as - *the state of an object represents the cumulative results of its behaviour.*
- *Identity* – The *identity* of an object is that property which distinguishes it from all other objects.

Question #13

List the possible operations that are performed on an object.

Answer

The kind of operations that are performed on objects comprises:

- *Modifier* – An operation that alters the state of an object.
- *Selector* – An operation that access the state of the object but does not alter it.
- *Iterator* – An operation that permits all parts of an object to be accessed in some well-defined order.
- *Constructor* – An operation that creates an object and/or initializes its state.
- *Destructor* – An operation that frees the state of an object and/or destroys the object itself.

Question #14

What are the possible relationships that exist between objects?

Answer

Objects contribute to the behaviour of a system by collaborating with one another. The relationship between any two objects encompasses the assumptions that each make about the other, including what operations can be performed and what behaviour results.

Objects communicate with each other through links, where a link defined as a physical or a conceptual connection between objects.

As a participant in a link, an object may play one of the following roles:

- *Client/Actor* – that operate on other objects, but is never operated upon by other objects.
- *Server* – that never operates upon other objects, it is only operated upon by other objects.
- *Agent* – that can operate on other objects and be operated upon by other objects; an agent is usually created to do some work on behalf of an actor or another agent.

Question #15

What does interface of a class represent?

Answer

The interface of a class represents outside view of a class and encompasses the abstraction while hiding its structure and the secrets of its behaviour.

This interface primarily consists of the declarations of all the operations applicable to instances of this class, but it may include the declarations of other classes, constants, variables, and exceptions that are needed to complete the abstraction.

Interface of a class is divided into following parts:

- *Public* – A part that is accessible to all clients.
- *Protected* – A part that is accessible to the class and its subclasses.
- *Private* – A part that is accessible to the class only.

Different object-oriented programming languages provide different mixtures of *public*, *protected*, and *private* parts, which developers can choose among to establish specific access rights for each part of the class's interface, and thereby exercise control over what clients can see and what they cannot see.

Question #16

What does implementation of a class represent?

Answer

Implementation of a class represents inside view of a class that encompasses the secrets of its behaviour. It primarily consists of implementation of all the operations defined in the interface of the class.

Question #17

What is the advantage of separating an interface from the implementation of a class?

Answer

By separating implementation of a class from its interface, we have the flexibility of changing its implementation.

Popular technologies, such as Component Object Model (COM) and Enterprise Java beans (EJB), are based on this facet of object-oriented programming.

Question #18

What is abstraction?

Answer

Dictionary meaning of word *abstraction* refers to the act of emphasizing and representing essential features and ignoring the irrelevant features. In the context of object-oriented programming, word *abstraction* refers to the separation between the specification of data and its implementation.

It results in better quality programs and more efficient programming techniques. These, in turn, reduce the number of man-hours required to develop a software system, and hence reduce the total cost of the final software product.

Since classes use the concept of data abstraction, they are also known as *abstract data types* (ADTs).

Question #19

What is encapsulation?

Answer

Encapsulation is the concealing of the implementation details of a data object from the outside world. The data and functions are wrapped into a single unit, called *class*. Encapsulation is the most striking feature of a class.

Question #20

Give a real life example to demonstrate the use of abstraction and encapsulation.

Answer

The notion of abstraction and encapsulation are commonly used in human-machine interaction and are widely prevalent in the technology-oriented world in which we are living.

Consider, for example, the Video Cassette Player (VCP), which is an integral part of every household today. We make two observations about how VCPs are packaged and used.

- All our interactions with a VCP are made through buttons on the control panel such as PLAY, FF (forward), REW (rewind), REC (record), STOP, EJECT, etc.
- The VCP is packaged in such a way that we cannot interact directly with the internal circuitry. So, the *internal representation* of the VCP is *hidden* from the user. This is the principle of *encapsulation*.
- The instruction manual that accompanies the VCP tells us what the VCP is supposed to do if we press a particular button. It does not tell us how it is implemented inside the VCP. For example, it does not explain the sequence of electronic and mechanical events that result when the REW button is pressed. So, the instruction manual makes a clear distinction between what the VCP does and how it does. This distinction is the principle of *abstraction*.

Question #21

What is data hiding?

Answer

Data hiding deals with visibility of the members. The level of visibility determines which parts of the code can access the member.
All most all the object-oriented programming languages provide three levels of visibility – *private*, *protected*, and *public*.

Private members are accessible to members of the class only.

Protected members are accessible to members of the class and members of the derived class.

Public members are accessible from everywhere.

Question #22

What is inheritance?

Answer

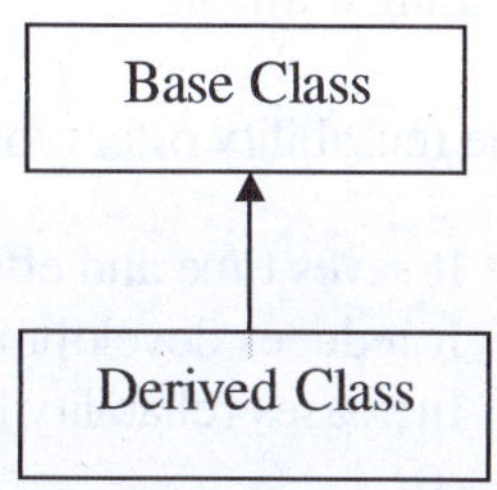

Inheritance is the process of creating new class(es), called *derived class(es)*, from existing class(es), called *base class(es)*. The derived class inherits all the features and capabilities of the base class(es) and can either refine some of its features or add new features of its own.

A number of terms are used to describe classes that are related through inheritance. A base class is often called the *ancestor*, *parent* or *superclass*. The derived class is called *descendent*, *child* or *subclass*.

Question #23

Whether private member are inherited or not?

Answer

Private members are inherited, but they cannot be accessed directly by the derived class. Only member functions of the class can access the private members. However, if the derived class member function wants to access the private member of the base class, it can do so indirectly by calling the member function of the base class.

Question #24

Explain the usefulness of inheritance?

Answer

The concept of inheritance provides reusability, *i.e.*, we can add new features to an existing class without modifying it. The new class will have combined features of base class and its own.

You know that it is always nice if we can reuse something that already exists instead of creating it afresh.

The reusability offers following advantages:

- It saves time and effort.
- It reduces development cost of new software product.
- Increases reliability because the class is already tested and used many times.

Question #25

Explain the possible types (forms) of inheritance?

Answer

The derived class inherits some or all of the features of the base class depending on the visibility mode and level of inheritance. Level of inheritance refers to length of its (derived class) path from the root (top base class). Remember that a base class itself may have been derived from other classes in the hierarchy.

Inheritance is classified into the following forms based on the levels of inheritance and interrelation among the classes involved in the inheritance process:

❑ *Single Inheritance*

Derivation of a single class from only one base class. The class *X* is the base class and *Y* is the derived class. Further no class is derived from *Y*.

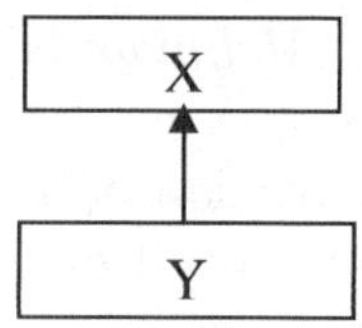

❑ *Multilevel Inheritance*

Derivation of a class from another derived class. The class *X* is the top base class and *Y* is the derived class of *X*. Further class *Z* is derived from class *Y*. Here, class *Y* is not just derived class, but also base class for class *Z*. Further, class *Z* can be used as base class for further derivation.

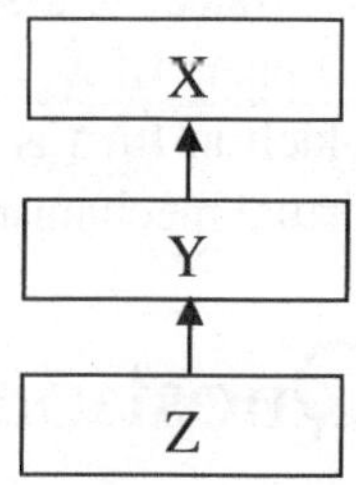

❑ *Multiple Inheritance*

Derivation of a class from two or more base classes. The class *X* and class *Y* are base classes and class *Z* is the derived class. Class *Z* inherits properties of both class *X* and class *Y*. Further, no class is derived from class *Z*.

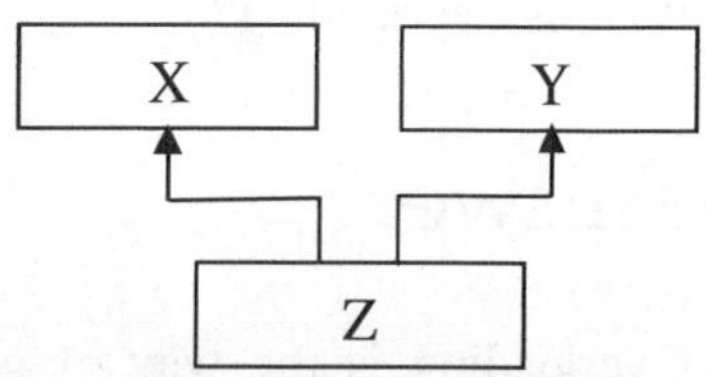

❑ *Hierarchical Inheritance*

Derivation of two or more classes from a single base class. Class *W* is the only base class and classes *X*, *Y* and *Z* are derived classes. Further, none of the class *X*, *Y* and *Z* is used as base class.

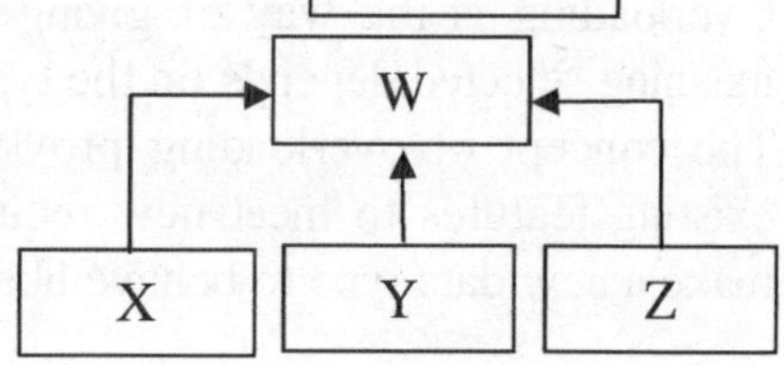

- *Hybrid Inheritance*

Derivation of a class involving two or more forms of inheritance. In this case, multilevel and multiple inheritances are involved. Class *Y* is derived from class *X*. It is a single type of inheritance. Further, derived class *Y* acts as a base class. The class *Z* is derived from classes *Y* and *W*. This type of inheritance that uses more than one base class is called multiple inheritance.

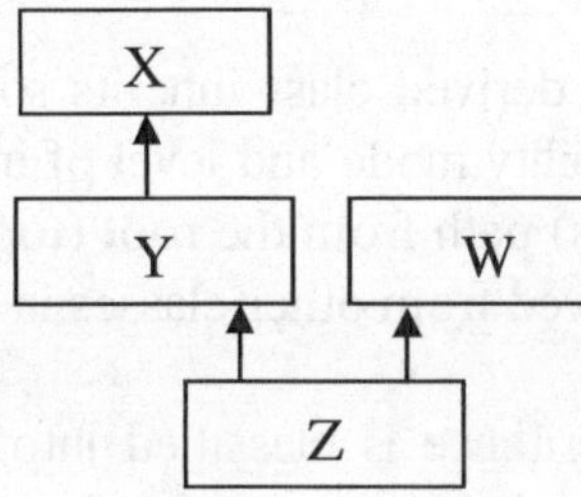

- *Multipath Inheritance*

Derivation of a class from two or more classes that are derived from the same base class. Class *X* is the base class. Classes *Y* and *W* are derived from base class *X*. Further, class *Z* is derived from classes *Y* and *W*. Since, classes *Y* and *W* have inherited same members of *X*. In this case, an ambiguity is generated which in turn is resolved using virtual keyword. The virtual mechanism is explained later.

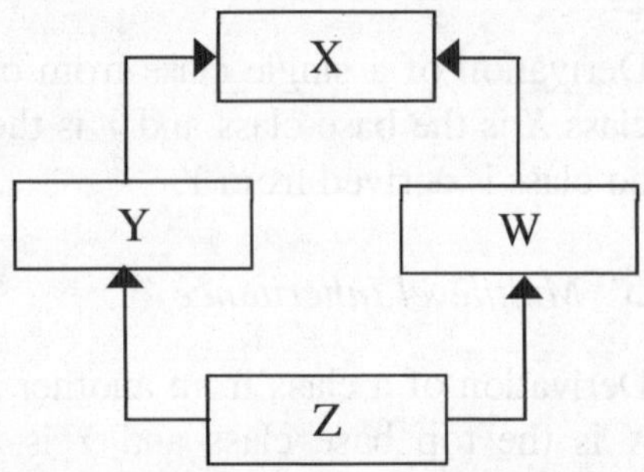

Question #26

What is overloading?

Answer

Overloading is the way of giving several meanings to an operator or a function. The meaning selected depends on the types of the arguments used by an operator or a function. The concept of overloading provides extensibility. This means that we can extend the existing features to meet new requirements. For example, by overloading operators, we make a new data type to behave like a built-in data type.

Question #27

What is polymorphism?

Answer

Polymorphism is a combination of two words *poly* and *morphism*. The word *poly* means *many* and the word *morphism* means *forms*.

Thus, *polymorphism* means *many forms*. More formally, polymorphism can be defined as a technique that allows defining various forms of a single function or operator that can be shared by various objects to perform the operation.

The polymorphism is achieved using the following:

- Function overloading
- Operator overloading
- Dynamic binding (virtual functions)

Question #28

What is dynamic binding?

Answer

Binding is the linking of a function call to the function definition that will be executed on the call during program execution. Normally the function call is tied to the function definition during the linking process. This process is known as *early binding*.

However, the OOP permits dynamic binding, also called *late binding*, where the tie-up of function call to the address code is delayed until the run-time.

Question #29

What is messaging?

Answer

An object-oriented program consists of set of objects that communicate with each other in order to solve a particular problem. Objects communicate with one another by sending and receiving information much the same way as people pass messages to one another. A message for an object is a request for execution of a function, and therefore will invoke a function in the receiving object that generates the desired results. Message passing involves specifying the name of the object, the name of the function and the information to be sent.

Every object has a life cycle – they are created and destroyed. Communication with an object is feasible as long as it is alive.

Question #30

What is the difference between an object-based language and object-oriented language?

Answer

Languages that support only objects and classes are called object-based languages. Such languages do not support features like inheritance and polymorphism. These languages only allow you to create objects and call methods using these objects. Visual Basic (VB) language is an example of object-based language.

On the other hand, object-oriented languages support full range of object-oriented concepts including inheritance and polymorphism. Java, C++, C#, Visual C++ (VC++) languages is example of object-oriented languages.

Question #31

What is UML?

Answer

UML (Unified Modeling Language) is a modeling language used in designing object models for software applications. It helps to specify, visualize and document models of software systems.

Question #32

What are different UML diagrams?

Answer

UML defines a total of 12 diagrams which are grouped into following three categories:

- *Structures diagrams* – These diagrams include class diagram, object diagram, component diagram and deployment diagram.
- *Behavior diagrams* – These diagrams include use case diagram (used during requirement gathering), sequence diagram, activity diagram and collaboration diagram.
- *Model management diagrams* – These diagrams include packages, subsystems and models.

Question #33

What is a class diagram?

Answer

A class diagram in UML is a type of static structure diagram that describes the structure of a system by showing the system's classes, their attributes, operations (or methods), and the relationships among the classes.

The class diagram is the main building block of object oriented modeling. It is used both for general conceptual modeling of the systematics of the application, and for detailed modeling translating the models into programming code.

Class diagrams can also be used for data modeling. The classes in a class diagram represent both the main objects and/or interactions in the application and the objects to be programmed.

In class diagram, a class is represented with boxes which contain three parts:

BankAccount
String owner float balance
deposit (float amount) withdrawal (float amount)

- Upper part holds the name of the class.
- Middle part contains the attributes of the class.
- Bottom part gives the methods or operations the class can take or undertake.

Question #35

What are design principles?

Answer

Software design principles represent a set of guidelines that helps us to avoid having a bad design. According to Robert Martin there are three important characteristics of a bad design that should be avoided:

- *Rigidity* - It is hard to change because every change affects too many other parts of the system.
- *Fragility* - When you make a change, unexpected parts of the system break.
- *Immobility* - It is hard to reuse in another application because it cannot be disentangled from the current application.

Question #36

What is Open Close Principle (OCP)?

Answer

It simply states that software entities like classes, modules and functions should be open for extension but closed for modifications.

OCP is a generic principle. You can consider it when writing your classes to make sure that when you need to extend their behavior you don't have to change the class but to extend it. The same principle can be applied for modules, packages, libraries. If you have a library containing a set of classes there are many reasons for which you will prefer to extend it without changing the code that was already written (backward compatibility, regression testing, etc.). This is why we have to make sure our modules follow OCP.

When referring to the classes, OCP can be ensured by use of Abstract Classes and concrete classes for implementing their behavior. This will enforce having Concrete Classes extending Abstract Classes instead of changing them. Some particular cases of this are Template Pattern and Strategy Pattern.

Question #37

What is Dependency Inversion Principle (DIP)?

Answer

It simply states that

- High-level modules should not depend on low-level modules. Both should depend on abstractions.
- Abstractions should not depend on details. Details should depend on abstractions.

This principle teaches us that we should decouple high level modules from low level modules, introducing an abstraction layer between the high level classes and low level classes. Further more it inverts the dependency, instead of writing our abstractions based on details, we should write the details based on abstractions.

Dependency Inversion or Inversion of Control is better known terms referring to the way in which the dependencies are realized. In the classical way when a software module (class, framework, etc.) need some other module, it initializes and holds a direct reference to it. This will make the 2 modules tight coupled. In order to decouple them the first module will provide a hook (a property, parameter, etc.) and an external module controlling the dependencies will inject the reference to the second one.

By applying the Dependency Inversion the modules can be easily changed by other modules just changing the dependency module. Factories and Abstract Factories can be used as dependency frameworks, but there are specialized frameworks for that, known as Inversion of Control Container.

Question #38

What is Interface Segregation Principle (ISP)?

Answer

It simply states that clients should not be forced to depend upon interfaces that they don't use.

This principle teaches us to take care how we write our interfaces. When we write our interfaces we should take care to add only methods that should be there. If we add methods that should not be there the classes implementing the interface will have to implement those methods as well. For example, if we create an interface called *Worker* and adds a method lunch break, all the workers will have to implement it. What if the worker is a *robot*?

As a conclusion, interfaces containing methods that are not specific to it are called *polluted* or *fat* interfaces. We should avoid them.

Question #39

What is Single Responsibility Principle (SRP)?

Answer

It simply states that a class should have only one reason to change.

In this context a responsibility is considered to be one reason to change. This principle states that if we have two reasons to change for a class, we have to split the functionality in two classes.

Each class will handle only one responsibility and on future if we need to make one change we are going to make it in the class which handles it. When we need to make a change in a class having more responsibilities the change might affect the other functionality of the classes.

Question #40

What is Liskov's Substitution Principle (LSP)?

Answer

It simply states that derived types must be completely substitutable for their base types.

This principle is just an extension of the OCP in terms of behavior meaning that we must make sure that new derived classes are extending the base classes without changing their behavior. The new derived classes should be able to replace the base classes without any change in the code.

Question #41

What are design patterns?

Answer

These are standard solutions for certain common problems that occur while designing a software system. For example, whenever we want restrict an application to create only one instance of a class, we can make use of the Singleton design pattern.

Various design patterns are divided into following three main categories:

- Creational
- Behavioral
- Structural

Question #42

Explain Singleton design pattern.

Answer

The Singleton design pattern is one of the simplest design patterns. It involves only one class which is responsible to instantiate itself, to make sure it creates not more than one instance. It provides a global point of access to that instance. The same instance can be used from everywhere, being impossible to invoke directly the constructor each time.

❑ ❑ ❑

Chapter 6

The C++ Language

Question #1

Enumerate some key differences between C and C++.

Answer

- C++ is a super set of C.
- C provides action/structure/function oriented programming whereas C++ provides Object-Oriented Programming with features like abstraction, encapsulation, inheritance and polymorphism.
- C++ is a strong type checking language compared to C. So many programs that would compile without any warning or error on a C compiler might result in many warnings and errors on a C++ complier.
- C++ supports sophisticated error handling using the exception handling mechanism.

Question #2

In how many ways we can pass arguments to a function?

Answer

There are three ways in which we can pass arguments to a function:

- By value

```
void fun(int x, float y);     // function declaration
fun(a, b);                    // function call
```

- By address (pointer)

```
void fun(int *x, float *y);   // function declaration
fun(&a, &b);                  // function call
```

- By reference

```
void fun(int& x, float& y);   // function declaration
fun(a, b);                    // function call
```

Question #3

What are the advantages of passing arguments to a function by reference or address over passing by value?

Answer

- The first advantage is that we are able to modify the actual variable from the called functions.
- The second advantage is that you can avoid creation of new variable(s) in the function. For example, when you pass a large structure by value, a new structure variable of the same size is created in the function which consumes memory. When you pass such a structures by reference or by pointer then only a reference or pointer variable occupying 2 or 4 bytes will be created.

Question #4

What is an inline function?

Answer

The function whose code (definition) gets inserted at the function call rather than resulting in a transferring control (jumping) to the function definition at the execution time.

Question #5

How can we make a function inline?

Answer

We can make a function inline by prefixing the function definition by the keyword *inline*.

By making the function inline, we request the compiler to insert the code at the place where there is a function call, so that, time is saved in calling the function and returning from the function. The compiler takes the decision whether to insert the code or not depending on the size of the code optimization settings of the compiler.

In situations, where a function with a small code is getting called several times, we can save the overhead involved in calling the function by making the function inline.

Question #6

What is the advantage of using the *inline* function?

Answer

An *inline* keyword before a function suggests the compiler to insert the complete body of the function wherever that function is invoked.

Inline expansion is typically used to eliminate the inherent cost involved in calling a function. It is typically used for functions that need quick execution.

Question #7

Can a function be forced as *inline*?

Answer

No. Inline expansion is purely at the hands of the complier. The complier can ignore your request if a particular function does not suit for inline expansion. C++ specification doesn't specify under what condition the complier will ignore the inline request.

Question #8

Compare *inline* function with the *macro*.

Answer

Macro invocations do not perform type checking.

```
# include <iostream.h>
# define MULTIPLAY(a, b)     a * b
inline int mul(int a, int b)
{
    return (a+b);
}
void main()
{
    cout << MULTIPLY (1+2, 3+4));
    cout << mul(1+2, 3+4);
}
```

In the above example, the answer will be 11 and 21. Can you tell, Why?

Because the macro will be expanded as expression

```
1+2*3+4
```

Since * operator has higher precedence than + operator, the value will be 11 instead of 21.

To get the correct answer the macro should be declares as

```
# define MULTIPLY(a, b) (a) * (b)
```

This error wouldn't happen with the inline function.

Also,

- Compiler errors within macros are often difficult to trucks because they refer to the expanded code done by the processor program.
- Debugging the *inline* function is easier than that of macro-expanded code.

Question #9

What do you mean by function overloading?

Answer

Function overloading is defining multiple functions with the same name. These functions must differ, in at least in one of the following - *number*, *order* or *types* of arguments.

Question #10

What is the advantage of function overloading?

Answer

C++ allows function overloading wherein the programmer can create three different functions with the same name but with different types of arguments as shown below:

```
void swap(int, int);
void swap(float, float);
void swap(double, double);
```

With function overloading we are relieved from remembering different function names just because their arguments are different.

Question #11

Can a function be overloaded based on return types?

Answer

No. Function signature does not depend on the return type. So, overloading can't be resolved by the return type alone.

Question #12

Why function overloading does not depended on the return type of the function?

Answer

This can be explained with the help of following example:

```
#include <iostream.h>
int f()
{
    // code;
}
void f()
{
    // code;
}
void main()
{
     // code
     f();        // ambiguity
     y = f();   // ambiguity
     // more code
}
```

There is an ambiguity in the function call because the compiler will not be able to figure out which version should be called. Even if we are not collecting the value we cannot assume the function *f()* that does not return would get called. This is because it not necessary to collect the returned value even if the called function returns a value.

Question #13

How C++ manages function overloading?

Answer

Global function (functions that are not members of any class) and non-virtual member functions of a class are always called by name. Since overloaded functions have the same name it would become impossible to call different versions of the same function. Hence, C++ compiler changes names of all the function definition and calls during compilation. This process is known as *name mangling*. Name mangling is also known as name decoration.

Question #14

What is name mangling?

Answer

Name mangling mean assigning different names to different versions of an overloaded function. Compiler mangles name as per the type, order and number of arguments.

Name mangling is implementation dependent. Different compilers may be using slightly different mechanism.

Question #15

How name mangling can be prevented?

Answer

To prevent name mangling for a given function, declare the function with *extern "C"* attributes. Functions declared with *extern "C"* attribute are treated as C-style functions, hence the compiler does not mangle them.

This is shown below:

```
#include <iostream.h>
extern "C" void display()
{
    cout << "\nThis function will not be mangled . . .\n";
}
void main()
{
    display();
}
```

Question #16

What is a generic pointer?

Answer

A *generic pointer* is a kind of pointer that can be used to hold addresses of operands of different types at certain times. The syntax for declaring a generic pointer is

```
void *ptr;
```

Question #17

Are there any limitations of generic pointers?

Answer

Yes.

Though, a generic pointer is very versatile pointer, it suffers from following serious problems:

1. Generic pointers cannot be directly de-referenced. They need to appropriately type casted.
2. Pointer arithmetic cannot be performed on generic pointers.

The reason for both of these problems is that the compiler cannot determine the size of the operand whose address is held in the generic pointers.

Question #18

What is a pointer to a pointer?

Answer

A pointer is variable that holds the address of another variable. This concept can be further extended. We can have a variable that hold an address of a variable that in turn holds an address of another variable. This type of variable will be known as *pointer to a pointer.* The underlying concept is known as *double indirection.* This concept can be further extended to triple level, fourth level, and so on.

Question #19

Can you given a practical example to demonstrate the use of pointer to a pointer?

Answer

One such practical example of using pointers to pointers is when pointers are passed by address to a calling function. The following skeleton of code demonstrates this:

```
void main()
{
    int *ptr1;
    // . . .
    func1( &ptr1, . . . );
    // . . .
}
void func1( int **ptr2, . . . )
{
    // . . .
    func2( &ptr2 );
    // . . .
}
void func2( int ***ptr3, . . .)
{
    // . . .
    // . . .
}
```

Question #20

Can we have a pointer to a function? If yes, write an example program to demonstrate the use of pointer to function.

Answer

Yes. Every function has an address, and if we know the address of a function, we can access the function through its address. This provides another way of accessing a function. The syntax of declaring a pointer to a function is

```
type (*ptr) ( for-args );
```

where *type* is the return type of the function, and *for-args* is a list of formal arguments or list specifying types of formal arguments. The parentheses around **ptr* tells the compiler that it is a pointer to a function.

The function will be accessed as

```
(*ptr) (act-args);
```

where *act-args* is list of actual arguments. Before using this statement, it is assumed that the address of the function is assigned to variable *ptr*.

Following example illustrate the use of pointer to a function.

```
#include <iostream.h>
int maxx(int x, iny y)
{
   return ( x>y?x:y );
}

void main()
{
   int a = 10, b =20, c;
   int (*pf)(int,int);
   pf = maxx;
   c = (*pf)(a,b);
   cout << "\nc = " << c << "\n";
}
```

Question #21

What is static memory allocation?

Answer

When you give a command to run your program, the operating system allocates a block of memory for your program, loads it from the secondary storage (Floppy disk, hard disk, CD or DVD, etc.) into that block and then initiates its execution.

When the program finishes its execution, the memory occupied by the program is automatically released. It means that the memory requirements are determined prior to execution of your program, and thereafter your program neither can acquire more memory nor can release the free memory, if not required.

The above situations depicts a situation where the amount of memory required is known before hand, and the compiler then can determine the memory requirements for the data as well as the instructions. In such a situation, memory allocation is known as *static memory allocation*.

Question #22

What is dynamic memory allocation?

Answer

It is important to note that the memory requirements for the instructions are always fixed. However, there may be situation when the exact memory requirements for the data may not be known in advance or the data requirements may vary from one program execution to another program execution, *i.e.*, memory requirements for the data are dynamic.

Therefore, when the amount of memory is not known before hand for a particular data item(s), then it is allocated at the execution time, *i.e.*, when the program is running. In such a situation, memory allocation is known as *dynamic memory allocation*.

Question #23

Differentiate between static memory allocation and dynamic memory allocation.

Answer

In simple terms static memory allocation is the allocation of memory at compile time where as the dynamic memory allocation is the allocation of memory at execution time (run-time).

Question #24

What is a heap or free store?

Answer

Every program is provided with a pool of unallocated memory that it can utilize during execution. This pool of unallocated memory is known as *heap* or *free store*.

Therefore, whenever the memory of requisite size (amount) is required by the program, it is taken from the free store, and when the previously allocated memory is not required further, it is returned back to the free store.

Question #25

How dynamic memory is managed in C++?

Answer

Dynamic memory in C++ can be managed using either of the following:

- Memory management functions { *malloc*(), *calloc*(), *realloc*() and *free*() }
- Memory management operators (*new* and *delete*)

Table 6.1: Memory management functions

Name	Description
malloc	Allocates memory from heap.
calloc	Allocates memory from heap and initializes the allocated memory to zeroes.
realloc	Readjusts the existing block and copies the contents to the new location.
free	Deallocates a block allocated by *malloc*, *calloc* and *realloc* functions.
coreleft	Returns a measure of unused memory.

Table 6.2: Memory management operators

Name	Description
new	Allocates memory from heap.
delete	Deallocates a block allocated *new* operator.

Note:

Never mix the use of memory management functions and memory management operators.

If the memory is allocated using memory management functions, it should be deleted with *free*() function only not with *delete* operator.

Similarly, if the memory is allocated using *new* operator, it should be deleted with *delete* operator only not with *free*() function.

Question #26

What is the difference between the working of *malloc*() function and *new* operator?

Answer

<u>Working of *malloc*() Function:</u>

- Allocates requisite amount of memory and returns a generic pointer which needs to be casted to appropriate type.
- In case sufficient memory is not available, it returns a NULL pointer.

Working of *new* Operator:

- Allocates requisite amount of memory and returns a pointer of appropriate type, and thus no casting is required.
- In case sufficient memory is not available, it returns throws a *bad_alloc* exception.
- When an object is created using *new* operator, i.e., dynamically, after memory is allocated for the object, it automatically calls the destructor.

Question #27

What is the difference between the working of *free*() function and *delete* operator?

Answer

In dealing with built-in data types, there is no difference. But when dealing with objects, they work differently. The *free*() function just deallocates the memory, whereas the *delete* first calls the destructor and then deallocates the memory.

Question #28

Suppose *objs* is a pointer to a dynamically created array of objects, which of the following statement is correct way to delete the array *objs*?

```
delete abjs;
delete [] objs;
```

Answer

The correct way is

```
delete [] objs;
```

The reason being is that in the first statement, destructor will only be invoked on the first object before deleting the array, where as in the second, destructor will be called on every object before deleting the entire array.

Question #29

Suppose *a* is a pointer to a dynamically created array, when array is deleted using either *malloc*() function or *delete* operator, what happens to the pointer?

Answer

Nothing, pointer retains it value (address). Only block of memory allocated for array is deleted.

Question #30

Suppose *a* is a pointer to a dynamically created array, when array is deleted using either *malloc*() function or *delete* operator, whether pointer variable is deleted or block of memory allocated for array is deleted of both gets deleted?

Answer

Only block of memory allocated for array is deleted. Pointer variable remains intact and its value also remain un-effected.

Question #31

Recall that when we use *free()* function or *delete* operator to deallocate the dynamiccaly allocated block, we only pass pointer to the block, then how *free()* function or *delete* operator know how many bytes it should deallocate?

Answer

When operating system allocates memory, on call to *malloc()*, *calloc()*, *realloc()* functions or *new* operator, to a program from its free pool of memory (also called free store), it keeps track of the address of the block and the size of the block.

Therefore, when the memory needs to be deallocated, the program need only to tell the address of the block to the operating system.

Question #32

Can we increase the size of the dynamically allocated array?

Answer

Yes. This can be done using the *realloc()* function.

Question #33

What possible problems can occur while working with pointers?

Answer

While working with pointers, following possible problems can occur:

- Problem of dangling/wild pointers.
- Problem of memory leaks.
- Problem of NULL pointer assignment.
- Problem of allocation failures.

Question #34

What is a dangling/wild pointer?

Answer

It is a pointer that is not initialized with a valid address. Such a pointer can end up pointing anywhere in memory that may include the program code itself or to the code of the operating system. The use of such pointer can lead to undesirable results. Therefore, care must be taken to initialize pointers with valid address before use.

Question #35

What is a memory leak?

Answer

It is a situation where the programmer fails to release the memory allocated at run time in a module. Remember that when memory is allocated, a pointer variable is used to hold the address of the allocated block, however, when the module completes its execution, the pointer variable goes out of scope and there will be no way to reach that memory block.

Therefore, care must be taken to release the allocated memory block in a module where memory was allocated.

```
// Program to illustrate the cause of memory leak
#include <iostream.h>
void main()
{
    fun();          //  invoke function named 'fun'
}
void fun()
{
    int *intPtr;
    // allocate memory for 'n' integer numbers
    intPtr = new [n*sizeof(int)];
    //  work on the allocated block
}
```

Question #36

What is a NULL pointer assignment?

Answer

It is a situation that happens when a pointer points to address 0, which is called NULL. For example, it may happen that if the pointer variable is declared as global, since global variables are initialized to 0. Likewise, this can also happen for a local un-initialized pointer variable, particularly for local static variables, they are also initialized to 0. When it happens, and the pointer is used on the left-hand side of an assignment operator, the system generates a message "*Null pointer assignment*".

Question #37

What is an allocation failure?

Answer

It is a situation when the program through *malloc()*, *calloc()*, or *realloc()* function or new *operator* request for a block of memory, and the operating could not fulfill the request of the program because the sufficient memory may not be available in the free pool. In that case, these functions return a NULL pointer indicating the allocation failure.

Therefore, the programmer should take care of allocation failures and provide a safe exit in their programs on such failures.

```
// Program to illustrate the allocation failure, and
// the way it should be handled
#include <iostream.h>
void main()
{
    int *intPtr;
    //  allocate memory for 'n' integer numbers
    intPtr = new [n*sizeof(int)];
    if ( intPtr == NULL ) {
        cout << "\nUnable to allocate memory . . .\n";
        return;
    }
    //   work on the allocated block
    delete intPtr;    // release the memory
}
```

Question #38

What are the different Access Specifiers?

Answer

Class members can have either of the following access specifiers:

- *private* is the default access and private members are accessible only from the member functions of the same class and/or from their friends functions/classes.

- *protected* members are accessible from member functions of the same class and/or friend classes, and also from members of their immediate derived class.
- *public* members are accessible from anywhere the class is visible.

Question #39

How does a class differ from a structure in C++?

Answer

Structure	Class
Default access is public.	Default access is private.
Default inheritance type is public.	Default inheritance type is private.

Question #40

Can we initialize a data member in class template? If not, why?

Answer

No. When we declare a class, *i.e.*, create a template for a class, no memory is allocated, and hence it is not possible to initialize a data member in class template.

Question #41

Is there any restriction on the definition of the member functions inside the class template?

Answer

Yes. If body of the member function contain any kind of loop (using *for*, *while* or *do-while* statement), that member function cannot be defined inside the class template.

Note that the member functions defined inside the class template are *inline* by default. And any function involving loops cannot be inline, and hence can not be defined inside the class template.

Question #42

How can we make the member function defined outside the class template as inline?

Answer

By prefixing the function declarator statement with keyword *inline* as shown below

```
inline void Example::show()
{
     // body of the function
}
```

where *show()* is a member function of *Example* class.

Note that if a member function defined outside the class template contains a loop, it cannot be made *inline*. Doing so will cause a syntax error.

Question #43

How can we call member functions from outside the class?

Answer

To call a non-static member function from outside the class, we always need an object of that class. On the other hand, to call a static member either an object or class can be used.

Question #44

How can we initialize an array of objects?

Answer

This is explained with the help of example.

```
class Point2D {
    private:
       int x;
       int y;
    public:
       Point2D(int x1, int y1) {
           x = x1;
           y = y1;
       {
       // other members
};
void main()
{
    Point2D pts[5] = { Point2D(0,0), Point2D(2,7), Point2D(5,4),
                       Point2D(7,10), Point2D(9,8) };
    // other statements
}
```

Here *pts* is an array of *Point2D* objects. To initialize the array we are required to create those many objects and assign their values to the elements of the array.

Question #45

Does member functions are counted while computing the size of an object?

Answer

No. Though it seems that objects contain data members as well as member functions but actually they contain data members not the member functions.

Each objects carries its own copy of data members, however, they share the member functions. Therefore, there will be one set of data members for each object but only one copy of the member functions that is stored in separate area of computer memory.

Question #46

Consider following class template

```
class Example {
    private:
        int x;
    public:
        Example(int a)  {
            x = a;
        }
        // other member functions
};
```

Can we create an object named *obj* of the class *Example* through following statement?

```
Example obj = 10;
```

Answer

Yes.

Compiler will treat the statement

```
Example obj = 10;
```

as

```
Example obj(10);
```

Therefore, one-argument constructor will be invoked. If compiler could not find one-argument constructor, it will flag an error message.

Question #47

Consider following class template

```
class Example {
    private:
        int x;
        int y;
    public:
        Example(int a, int b) {
            x = a;
            y = b;
```

```
        }
        // other member functions
};
```

Can we create an object named *obj* of the class *Example* through following statement?

```
Example obj = 10, 20;
```

Answer

No. Compiler will flash an error message, as this syntax works only on one-argument constructor not on constructors with two or more arguments.

Question #48

What is the size of an object of an empty class?

Answer

The size of an object of empty class is one byte. Since C++ allows us to define objects of an empty class, it should have some bytes of memory.

The minimum amount of memory that could be reserved is 1 byte. Hence the object size of an empty class turns out be 1 byte.

Question #49

How a member function comes to know on which object it is invoked and hence has to work?

Answer

Whenever a member function is invoked on an object, address of the object gets passed to the member function implicitly. This address gets collected in the *this* pointer through which the function can know on which object it invoked and thus has to work on.

Question #50

What is *this* pointer and what is its type?

Answer

The *this* pointer is a special pointer which collects the address of the object on which member function is called. If *Example* is the name of the class, then type of the *this* pointer will be

```
Example* const this;
```

It acts as a constant pointer, and hence its contents cannot be modified.

Question #51

When does the *this* pointer gets created?

Answer

The *this* pointer gets created when a member function (non-static) of a class is called.

Question #52

Can we create an object dynamically?

Answer

Yes. The memory management operator *new* allow us to create object dynamically as shown in the following code snippet

```
Example *ptr = new Example(10);
```

Here *Example* is class having single argument constructor. The *new* operator creates an object dynamically and returns the address of the newly created object which is assigned to pointer variable *ptr*.

Question #53

How can we call a member function through a pointer to an object?

Answer

To call a member function through a pointer to an object, we use arrow operator '->' as shown below

```
Example *ptr = new Example(10);
ptr->fun();
```

where *ptr* is a pointer to an object of class *Example* and *fun()* is a member function of class *Example*.

Question #54

How can we destroy a dynamically object?

Answer

This task is accomplished using the *delete* memory management operator. The *delete* operator first invokes the destructor and then releases the memory occupied by the object that was previously allocated by new operator.

Example

```
Example *ptr = new Example(10);
// some code here

delete ptr;
```

Question #55

What is the difference between the following two statements if *a* is a pointer to an array of objects allocated dynamically?

```
delete a;
delete [] a;
```

Answer

First statement will invoke destructor on the first object before deleting the entire array.

Second statement will invoke destructor on every object before deleting the entire array.

Question #56

What is a static member of a class?

Answer

Static member of class is that member whose declaration is preceded with a keyword *static*. These members belong to the entire class.

Irrespective of the number of object only one copy of the static data member is maintained and is shared by all the objects.

A static member function can access only the static data members not the non-static data members.

Question #57

When we need to use static data members in a class?

Answer

Static data members are needed when some data is to be shared among the objects of a class.

For example, in a program each object may want to know how many objects are active in the program. To accomplish such a task one static data member, say *count*, can be used whose value will indicate the active objects at a given time.

Whenever a new object is created *count* is incremented in the constructor of the class and when ever an object is destroyed the *count* is decremented in the destructor of the class.

Question #58

Can we initialize a static data member in a constructor of a class?

Answer

Note that a static data member belongs to the entire class not to an individual object, and a constructor is executed when a new object of the class is created.

Further, even if the initialization of the static data member is permitted, every time a new object is created the static data member would always be initialized, and therefore it will loose its current value.

Question #59

How static data member is initialized?

Answer

Note that a static data member is just declared in the class template, it has to be defined outside the class template.

It is always defined before the main function as shown below:

```
class Test
{
    private:
       static int count;
       int y;
    public:
       Test() {
          count++;
       }
```

```
        // other member functions
};
int Test::count = 0;    // initialize static data member
void main()
{
    // statements
}
```

Question #60

How *const* data member is initialized?

Answer

A *const* data member cannot be initialized inside the body of a constructor. It can only be initialized through an initializer list, as shown in the following code snippet:

```
class Test
{
    private:
        const int t;
    public:
        Test(int i) : t(i)
        { }
        // other member functions
};
void main()
{
    Test obj(10);
}
```

Question #61

What is an abstract class?

Answer

These are the classes, which are not complete and cannot be used to create objects. These classes contain at least one pure virtual function. These classes are used as framework upon which new classes can be built to provide new functionality.

Question #62

What is a friend function? How friend functions are useful?

Answer

A friend function is a non-member function (global function or member function of a class) that is declared as a friend of given class.

Consider a situation, where you want a function to operate on objects of two or more classes in order to manipulate their private data. One possible solution is to make this function member function of every class. The other alternative, and better in design, is to define the function as global function and make it friend of the class so that it can gain access to class's private data.

Question #63

What are the characteristics of a friend function?

Answer

A friend function has following characteristics:

- It can be declared in public or private section of the class without affecting its meaning.
- It is not in the scope of the class to which it has been declared as friend.
- It cannot access the members directly. To access members, it uses object and dot operator.
- It takes objects of classes as arguments.

Question #64

What is a constructor?

Answer

A *constructor* is a special member function that enables an object to initialize itself when it is created. This process is known as *automatic initialization*.

A constructor is automatically invoked when an object of its associated class is created. It is called constructor because it constructs object with its initial state by assigning initial values to it data members.

Question #65

Is it mandatory that every class must have constructor?

Answer

Yes. It is mandatory for every class to have at least one constructor. If the programmer has not defined any constrictor for the class, the compiler inserts one constructors of following form

```
ClassName() {}
```

called *default constructor*, which does nothing, and the data members will be undefined, i.e., take garbage values.

Question #66

What is a default constructor?

Answer

In case no constructor is defined by the programmer for a class, then compiler automatically inserts one constructor in the class definition prior to compiling the class.

This constructor has following structure

```
ClassName() {}
```

Note that this constructor takes no arguments and does nothing as it carries no statements. You must be thinking that *what values will be assigned to the object when the object is created using the default constructor*? The garbage (unpredictable) values will be assigned to the object.

Question #67

What is a zero-argument constructor?

Answer

Zero argument constructor is a kind of constructor that takes no arguments. It is used to initialize the every created object to a same specific state, *i.e.*, same initial values for all objects. This constructor has the following form

```
className()
{
    datamemeber1 = value1;
    datamemeber2 = value2;
            :
}
```

Question #68

What is the difference between default constructor and zero-argument constructor?

Answer

The only difference between default constrictor and zero-argument constructor is that default constructor does nothing (carries no statement) whereas the zero-argument constructor initializes the data member to specific predetermined values.

Example:

```
SampleClass()
{ }
```

```
SampleClass()
{
    a = 5;
    b = 7;
}
```

The first constructor (default) does nothing whereas the second constructor (zero-argument) initializes data member *a* to 5 and data member *b* to 7.

Question #69

What is a copy constructor?

Answer

A constructor that takes a single argument which is of its won class type.

It finds its use in the following situations:

- To create a new object of a class from its another existing object.
- To pass an object as an argument to its member function.
- To return an object from its member functions.

Example:

```
class Point2D
{
    private:
        int x;
        int y;
    public:
        Point2D(Point2D &ref)
        {
            x = ref.x;
            y = ref.y;
        {
        // other members
};
```

Question #70

What is *this* pointer? Where it finds its use?

Answer

The *this* pointer is a special pointer which is automatically created when a member (non-static) function is called on an object, and is implicitly passed to the member function. It acts as a constant pointer whose contents cannot be modified and its value represents the address of the object.

It is primarily used inside the member functions to resolve the scope of the data members when they share the name with formal arguments to the said member function.

Question #71

What is an initializer list?

Answer

An initializer list is a list that consists of data member name followed by argument name enclosed in parenthesis. This list is placed after the function declarator and before the function body as shown in following *Example* class template.

```
class Example
{
    private:
        int a;
        int b;
        int c;
   public:
        Example(int i,int j,int k) : a(j), b(i), c(k) { }
   void show() {
        // . . .
   }
 };
```

When constructor is invoked, the actual arguments are collected in formal arguments *i*, *j* and *k*. These values are then collected in data members *a*, *b* and *c*, respectively. This happens even before the constructor start executing.

Question #72

Can you cite a situation where the initializer list is indispensable?

Answer

The initializer list is indispensable when a data member is *const*. A *const* data member cannot be initialized in the body of the constructor. An attempt of doing so will be treated as an attempt of modifying the value of a *const* and compiler will flag a syntax error.

Question #73

What is the difference between a copy constructor and assignment operator?

Answer

The assignment operator assigns one object to another bit by bit, where as the copy constructor assigns one object to another member by member.

Question #74

Does the compiler provide a copy constructor in case the programmers don't provide it?

Answer

Yes. The copy constructor is used to copy an object into another of the same type at the time of initialization. Hence, it gets called when an object is passed to a function or returned from the function by value. So the compiler, by default, always provides a copy constructor in a class.

Question #75

What will happen if the argument is accepted by value in the copy constructor?

OR

Is it necessary to accept a reference the copy constructor?

Answer

If the argument is accepted by value in the copy constructor, the copy constructor will fall into recursive loop. This can be explained by the following example

```
class Example
{
    private:
        int x;
    public:
        Example()  {
            x = 10;
        }
        Example( Example p )
        {
            x = p.x;
        }
        void show()
        {
            cout << "\x = " << x << endl;
        }
};
void main()
{
    Example s1;
    Example s2(s1);
}
```

When the statement

```
Example s2(s1);
```

is executed, the copy constructor gets called and the value of object *s1* gets collected in *p*. This task is accomplished internally as

```
Example p = s1;
```

Here *p* is getting and initialized, and therefore, again the copy constructor would get called. This would result into recursive calls.

Question #76

Can static data member be initialized inside a constructor?

Answer

No. Note that the static data members belong to class not to the object, and constructor is invoked every time new object is created. If the initialization of static data members would have been allowed, it would always be reset. To avoid this situation, C++ system does not allow initialization of static data members in the body of a constructor.

Rather, a static data member is initialized before the *main()* function using syntax

```
int Example::count = 0:
```

Question #77

What is an explicit constructor?

Answer

An explicit constructor is a single argument constructor with *explicit* keyword prefixed with its name.

To understand its use consider the following *Sample* class template

```
class Sample {
    private:
        int a;
    public:
        Sample(int x){
            a = x;
        }
        // . . .
};
```

To create its object we can use either of the following statements

```
Sample obj(5);          //constructor invoked implicitly
Sample obj = Sample(5); //constructor invoked explicitly
```

However, the same object can also be created by using the following statement

```
Sample obj = 5;
```

This statement will automatically be converted in to a call to the *Sample* constructor with 5 being the argument, *i.e.*, the statement is handled by the compiler if it were written like

```
Sample obj(5);
```

However, if you do not want this implicit conversion to happen, you can prevent it by prefixing the keyword *explicit* before the single argument constructor as shown below:

```
class Sample {
    private:
        int a;
    public:
        explicit Sample(int x) {
            a = x;
        }
        // . . .
};
```

Now only statements like

```
Sample obj(5);   OR   Sample obj = Sample(5);
```

will work, and the statement like

```
Sample obj = 5;
```

will not be allowed. Doing so will cause a syntax error.

Question #78

What is a destructor?

Answer

A destructor, as its name implies, is a special member function that is used to release the resource held by the object before the object is destroyed. Like a constructor, the destructor also has the same name as that of class but is preceded by character tilde ('~'). For example, destructor for *ComplexNumber* class will be defined as

```
~ComplexNumber() { . . . }
```

Question #79

When is it mandatory for a class to have a destructor?

Answer

No. Destructor will be required in situations when certain resources, such as allocation of memory, creating a network connect, connecting to a database, etc., are allocated to the object during its creation (construction), which need to be returned/released before the object is destroyed (removed from memory). In the absence of a destructor, the object will die but the resources will not be returned to the pool of the operating system and hence will not be available for use by other applications/programs.

Question #80

Why destructors cannot be overloaded?

Answer

Destructor is invoked either when a statically allocated object goes out of scope or dynamically allocated object is deleted by using the *delete* operator.

Since destructor is invoked just before the object is destroyed, it makes no sense to pass arguments to a destructor which can then be used to assign to data members, and hence the C++ system does not allow overloading of destructors.

Question #81

Explain the usefulness of operator overloading.

Answer

Operator overloading allows exiting operators to operate on new data types the same way as they operate on the pre-defined data types. For example, by overloading binary addition ('+') operator on a class modeling a matrix, we will be to add two matrices the same way as we add two integers or floats.

For instance, if mat1, mat2, mat3 are three objects of matrix class, we will be able to add two matrices mat1 and mat2 and store its result in object mat3 by writing the following statement

```
mat3 = mat1 + mat2;
```

Question #82

What are the steps in overloading an operator?

Answer

The process of overloading involves the following steps:

- Create a class that defines a data type that is to be used for overloading an operator.
- Declare the *operator function op(argList)* in the public part of the class. It can be a member function or friend function.
- Define the operator function to implement the required operation.

Question #83

List the operators that cannot be overloaded. Also explain why they cannot be overloaded?

Answer

Operators that cannot be overloaded are '.', '.*', '::' and '?:'.

Operators '.' and '.*' are used to refer to the members of the class. They take name rather than value as their second operand. For example, when we write *p.a, a* is a name rather than a value, and *p.a* is the value. Since to an overloaded operator function, we must pass a value and not the name, and hence these operators cannot be overloaded.

Operator '::' refers to the variable not to a value to resolve the scope of the variable, hence it cannot be overloaded.

Even though '?:' is considered as operator (conditional operator or ternary operator), it does not perform an operation as such. It offers a compact way of representing a simple *if-else* statement, and hence it cannot be overloaded.

Question #84

While defining an operator function, the formal arguments are always either value variables or references. Why formal arguments as pointers are not permitted?

Answer

The situation can best be explained with the help of following example:

```
c = a + b;
```

where *a*, *b* and *c* are objects of example class, say *ComplexNumber*; and binary addition operator '+' is overloaded for it.

The above statement will be interpreted by the compiler as

```
c = operator + (a, b);
```

Here addresses of the variables are not passed, and therefore we cannot collect them in pointer variables. If we wish to collect them in pointer variables, the have to modify the statement as

```
c = &a + &b;
```

which gives the feeling that we are adding addresses and this leads to a meaningless situation, hence the collecting addresses in pointer variables is not permitted.

Question #85

How is it possible to distinguish between prefix and postfix notation while overloading increment '++' and decrement '—' operators?

Answer

By writing the keyword *int* as an argument, it possible to distinguish between prefix and postfix notation of increment and decrement operators.

```
class Counter
{
    private:
        int counterValue;
    public:
```

```
        void operator ++ ()   // prefix increment
        {
            ++counterValue;
        }
        void operator ++ (int)   // postfix increment
        {
            ++counterValue;
        }
};
```

Question #86

What is the usefulness of inheritance?

Answer

The usefulness of inheritance is in achieving reusability and extensibility. By reusability, we mean reusing something that already exists instead of creating it afresh. By extensibility, we mean extending the capabilities of something that already exists to incorporate new features.

Hence, we can say that inheritance is useful in following ways:

- It saves time and effort.
- It reduces development cost of new software product.
- Increases reliability because the class is already tested and used many times.

Question #87

What is the difference between *private*, *public*, and *protected* derivation?

Answer

- Incase of *private* derivation, the public and protected members of the base class become private members of the derived class.
- Incase of *public* derivation, the public members of the base class remain public members of the derived class. Similarly, the protected members of the base class remain protected members of the derived class.
- Incase of *protected* derivation, the public members of the base class become protected members of the derived class and protected members of the base class remain protected members of the derived class.

Question #88

Can a member function of a base class access any member of the derived class?

Answer

No. Only member functions of the derived class can access the members of the base class provided those member functions are either public or protected.

Question #89

In case of multiple inheritance, what is order of execution of constructors?

Answer

In case of multiple inheritance, the constructors are executed from the top base class downwards, i.e., the constructors of the top most base class in the hierarchy will be executed first and the constructor of the class whose object is being created will be executed at last.

Question #90

What is a virtual derivation? Where is it used?

Answer

The virtual derivation is a kind of derivation when we prefix the keyword *virtual* before the access specifier in the class derivation.

When more than one class is derived from the same base class, and these derived classes are further used in the derivation, it may cause ambiguity when a member that is prefix the keyword *virtual* before the access specifier in the class derivation. With virtual derivation, only single shared copy of the base class sub object is inherited regardless of how many times the base class occurs within the derivation hierarchy. The shared base class sub object is called *virtual base class*.

Question #91

What is the order of execution of constructors?

Answer

The order of execution of constructors is always as following:

1. *Base class constructor.* If there is more than base class, the constructors are executed in the order the base classes appear in the class derivation list, not in the order in which they are listed in the member initialization list. However, if there is a virtual base class in the class derivation list, its constructor will be executed first irrespective of its position the derivation list.
2. *Member class object constructor.* If there is more than one member class object, the constructors are executed in order the objects are declared in the class, not in the order in which they are listed in the member initialization list.
3. *Derived class constructor.*

Question #92

What is polymorphism? In what ways polymorphism can be achieved?

Answer

Polymorphism is a technique that allows to define various forms of a single function or operator that can be shared by various objects to perform the operations.

The polymorphism is achieved using the following:

- Overloading
- Dynamic binding

Question #93

What is static (early) and dynamic (late) binding?

Answer

The term binding refers to the linkage between a functional call and the function definition (the actual code that gets executed as a result of the call).

When this linkage is handled at the compile-time (by the compiler), it is called static (early) binding. It is early because it takes place before the execution of the program. It is static because it remains fixed and does not change at the execution time.

When this linkage is handled at the run-time (by the runtime), it is called dynamic (late) binding. It is late because it takes place during execution of the program. It is dynamic because it can change at the execution time.

Question #94

Can you give a real life example of static (early) and dynamic (late) binding?

Answer

Yes. The best real life example is of undertaking a journey by train and by air.

When you want to undertake journey by train, you need to book your ticket. This you can do in advance as the time permitted by the railways. When you book your ticket, you get a printed ticket with coach number and seat/birth number printed on it. It means that the seat/birth where you will sit is determined at the time you book your ticket, *i.e.*, before you actually undertake journey. This seat/birth number cannot be changed unless you get your ticket cancelled and book new one. This is analogous to static (early) binding in object-oriented programming.

When you want to undertake journey by air, you also need to book your ticket. This you can do in advance as the time permitted by the particular airways. When you book your ticket, you just get a printed ticket and the seat number is not mentioned on it. When you reach airport to catch the flight, you need to present your ticket at the airways counter which issues you a boarding pass that mentions your seat number. It means that the seat where you will sit is determined at the time you are ready to undertake your journey. This is analogous to dynamic (late) binding in object-oriented programming.

Question #95

What is a virtual function?

Answer

A member function whose function declaration is preceded by *virtual* keyword is known as a virtual function. These functions are defined in a base class in the public section and they provide a mechanism by which the derived classes can override it. These functions are bound dynamically.

The syntax for defining a virtual function is

```
class SampleClass
{
    private:
        . . . . .    // data members of the class
    public:
        . . . . .    // function members of the class
        virtual ReturnType FunctionName( agruments )
        {
            . . . . . // body of the virtual function
        }
};
```

At run time, it allows to decide which overridden form of the function is to used based on the type of object pointed by the base class pointer rather than the type of derived class pointer.

Question #96

What is a pure virtual function?

Answer

A pure virtual function is a virtual function with expression "= 0" appended to its declaration.

The syntax for defining a pure virtual function is

```
class BaseClass
{
    private:
        . . . . .   // data members of the class
    public:
        . . . . .   // function members of the class
        virtual ReturnType FunctionName(agruments) = 0;
};
```

A class with a pure virtual function is known as abstract (incomplete) class.

Question #97

What is VTABLE?

Answer

For every class that contains virtual functions, the compiler creates a VTABLE for each class and for class that is derived from it. The VTABLE contains the addresses of virtual functions in the order in which they virtual functions are defined within the class.

The address of VTABLE is stored in the pointer variable VPTR that is added in the beginning of an object.

Question #98

What is VPTR?

Answer

VPTR is a pointer variable that contains the address of the VTABLE. It is added in the beginning of an object.

Question #100

Whether there be is one VTABLE per object of a class or one VTABLE for the entire class?

Answer

There is only VTABLE for the entire class. All objects of a class share the same VTABLE. Each object contains the address of the VTABLE in its VPTR, a pointer variable that is added as a member in the beginning of the object.

Question #101

Are *this* pointer and VPTR are same?

Answer

No. The *this* pointer contains the address of the object where as VPTR contains the address of the VTABLE.

Question #102

Whether virtual function call works faster or slower than non-virtual (normal) function call?

Answer

Virtual function call works slower as compared to non-virtual (normal) function call as it involves retrieving the address of the virtual function from the VTABLE. Whereas the normal function is called directly.

Question #103

Does the virtual function of the base class which overridden in the base class also becomes?

Answer

Yes. All the virtual functions of the base class overridden in the drives class becomes virtual, and this applies to classes down the line in the class hierarchy.

Question #104

Can we declare a constructor as virtual?

Answer

No. It is not permitted. Note that the virtual mechanism works on the existence of objects, but no objects is available (exists) unless the constructor completes its execution. Thus it is meaningless to allow declaring constructor as virtual.

Question #105

What is a virtual destructor?

Answer

A destructor, in the base class, that is declared as virtual.

Note that when a destructor of the base class is declared a as virtual, the destructors of the derived classes automatically become virtual.

Virtual destructor ensures that the destructors are invoked in the right order in the class hierarchy when the objects are created dynamically using *new* operator.

Question #106

Is it necessary that the virtual function overridden in the derived class must have same signature?

Answer

Yes. If the virtual function of a base class is overridden in the derived class has different signature, *i.e.*, return type, number arguments or types of arguments differ, and then it becomes a new function.

Question #107

Is it necessary to override a virtual function?

Answer

No. We need to override the virtual function of a base class in the derive class only if the derived class want to define class specific behaviour.

When the virtual function of the base class is not overridden in the derived class, then the VTABLE of the derived class will contain the address of the base class virtual function.

Question #108

Can we redefine a virtual function of the base class as a non-virtual function in the derived class?

Answer

No. The virtual function can only be overridden in the derived class but cannot be made non-virtual.

Question #109

What are the different requirements to implement runtime polymorphism in C++?

Answer

The different requirements include:

- You need to have virtual functions in the base class.
- You need to have a pointer variable to base class.
- You need to store address of the object of the derived class in a pointer variable to base class.
- Invoke the function through the pointer to the base class.

Question #110

What is/are the drawback(s) of traditional error handling?

Answer

The major draw back of traditional error handling is that in some sense the code becomes polluted with the error processing. It becomes more difficult for a programmer concerned with the application itself to read the code and determine if the code is functioning correctly. This makes it more difficult to understand and to maintain the program.

Question #111

What is an exception? Give some reasons that cause exceptions.

Answer

Exceptions are errors that occur at run-time. Following are few reasons that cause exceptions:

- Division by zero.
- Square root or logarithm of a negative number.
- Unable to open a file.
- Insufficient memory.
- Array index out of bound, *i.e.*, outside the legal range.

Question #112

How we can handle exceptions?

Answer

C++ language provides three keywords – *try*, *throw* and *catch*, to handle exceptions.

The *try* keyword is used to preface the block of statements that may generate exception(s). This block of statements is known as *try block*. When an exception is detected, it is thrown using keyword *throw* in the try block. A *catch block* that is defined by prefacing a block of statement with *catch* keyword, catches the exception thrown by the throw statement in the try block, and handles it appropriately.

Following program skeleton shows program structure with exceptional handling features.

```
void main()
{
      . . . . .
      try {
            . . . . .   // statements which can cause,
            . . . . .   // detect and throw an exception
```

```
        throw exception;
        . . . . .
    }
    catch (DataType argument) {
        . . . . .       // statements that handles
        . . . . .       // the exception
    }
}
```

As soon as the *try block* throws an exception, the program control leaves the try block and enters the catch block. Note that exceptions are objects used to transmit information about a problem. If the type of the object thrown matches the data type of the *argument* in the catch statement, then catch block is executed for handling the exception. If they do not match, the program is aborted with the help of *abort()* function which is invoked by default. When no exception is detected, the control goes to the statement immediately after the catch block, *i.e.*, catch block is skipped.

Question #113

What is an exception handler?

Answer

It is a catch block that handles the runtime error. The catch block must appear just after the try block.

Question #114

What is the default exception handler?

Answer

It is the exception handler provided by the system, and when it is invoked it calls *terminate()* function which in turn invokes *abort()* function which ultimately terminates the program and displays the message "Abnormal program termination".

Question #115

What are the steps involved in exception handling?

Answer

Following are the four steps involved in exception handling:

1. Find the problem (*Hit the exception*).
2. Inform that an error has occurred (*Throw the exception*).
3. Receive the error information (*Catch the exception*).
4. Take corrective actions (*Handle the exception*).

Question #116

Is it possible to have try block in one functional unit and catch block in another functional unit of a program? Justify your viewpoint.

Answer

No. The requirements of exception handling demand that the catch block should immediately follow the try block, therefore, it is not possible to have try block in one functional unit and catch block in another functional unit of a program.

Question #117

Is it possible to have only one catch block to handle all possible exception? If yes, how?

Answer

Yes. By writing the catch block as shown below:

```
catch (...)
{
      // statements for handling all exception
}
```

It is always a good idea to use the *catch(. . .)* as a default statement along other catch handlers that it can catch all those exceptions which are not handled explicitly.

Question #118

Suppose we have built a class hierarchy, and using exception handling in our program with multiple catch blocks. If the type of the argument of first catch is of base class type, then what will happen when exceptions of all possible types are thrown?

Answer

Since argument for first catch block is base class type, it will catch all the exceptions thrown because an argument of the base class type substitutive all the class types in the hierarchy. Therefore, the control will never be transferred to other catch block despite of matching the exception and argument type of a particular block.

Question #119

What does re-throwing an exception mean? What purpose it can serve?

Answer

Re-throwing an exception is a situation where a handler may decide to throw the exception caught without or partially processing it. To re-throw an exception, simply invoke throw without any argument as shown below:

```
throw;
```

It causes the current exception to be thrown to the next enclosing try/catch sequence and is caught by a catch statement listed after that enclosing try block.

Question #120

Is it possible to restrict a function to throw only some specified exception? If yes how?

Answer

Yes. It is possible to restrict a function to throw only certain specified exceptions. This is achieved by adding a throw list clause to the function prototype/definition as shown below.

```
DataType functionName(argList) throw (excepList)
{
      . . . . .             // function body
      . . . . .
}
```

Throwing any other type of exception will cause abnormal program termination.

Question #121

Is it possible to stop a function from throwing any exception? If yes, how?

Answer

Yes. It is possible to stop a function from throwing any exception my making its exception list empty as shown below:

```
DataType functionName(argList) throw ()
{
      . . . . .             // function body
      . . . . .
}
```

Question #122

Suppose an exception is thrown, but there is no catch block to handle that exception then what will happen?

Answer

The default exception handler will be invoked that invokes *terminate()* function which in turn invokes *abort()* function which ultimately terminates the program and displays the message "Abnormal program termination".

Question #123

What is generic programming? How is it implemented in C++?

Answer

Generic programming is a kind of programming where a single code, either for function or class, is written to implement same functionality on different type of data.

Generic programming is implemented in C++ using templates –*function templates, class templates.*

We can write a single *function template* to sort an array and then C++ compiler will generate separate functions that will sort an array of *int*, sort an array of float, sort an array of double, etc.

Likewise, we can write a single *class template* for a stack class and then C++ compiler will generate separate classes such as stack of *int* class, stack of *float* class, etc.

Question #124

What are templates?

Answer

A template is a framework that allows us to write one function or class that works for different data types. By using templates, we can write a code for single class/function that operate on many data types, instead of having to write separate class/function for each type. When used with functions they are known as function templates and when used with classes they are known as class *templates.*

Question #125

How does a template work?

Answer

At compile time, the compiler simply remembers the function or class template for future use. For functions, the actual code is generated when the function is called with a specific data type. For classes, a new type specific class is created when an object using the template arguments is created.

Question #126

What is the difference between the function template and template function?

Answer

Consider the following code segment:

```
template <class T>
T FindMax(T a, T b)
{
    if ( a > b )
       return a;
    else
       return b;
}
```

The entire code segment is called the *function template*. Here data type is represented by a name *T* (it can be any other name as well), which is known as template argument.

When the function is called, it data specific code gets generated. This is called instantiating the function template. Each instantiated version of the function is called a *template function*.

Question #127

When should we use templates?

Answer

Templates are often used:

- To create a type-safe collection class, such as *stack*, that can operate on data of any type.
- An extra type checking for function that would otherwise take void pointers.

The above said tasks can be done even without templates, however, use of templates offers several advantages:

- Templates are easier to write. We can write only one generic version of our class or function instead of manually writing specific classes or functions.
- Templates are easier to understand, since they can provide a straightforward way of abstracting type information.
- Templates are type-safe, since the types that templates act upon are known at compile time, therefore the compiler can perform type checking before error occurs.

Question #128

Do templates provide reusability?

Answer

Yes. Templates provide a way to reuse the source code. Instead of writing type specific functions or classes, we write only one generic function or class that can work on any data type, and this significantly reduces code work and thus results in reduced effort and time of development, and in turn improves productivity.

Question #129

How do templates compare with macros?

Answer

Macros have very limited capability. They are usually used for functions for computing values. They are not type safe as no type checking can be performed by the pre-processor. They cannot be used for functions involving loops. Finally, macros are handled by pre-processor.

In contrast, a template can be used to substitute function providing full range of capability. They are type safe as the compiler can perform type checking. Templates are handled by the compiler.

Question #130

Distinguish between overloaded functions and function templates.

Answer

Overloaded functions are different definitions of the same function with different signatures, each one performing the same functionality on different data type. Compiler during compilation binds the function call with an appropriate function definition whose formal arguments and actual parameters match in type.

On the other hand, function template is a single definition of the function which can operate on different data types. Compiler during compilation first creates a definition of a function, from function template, for data type as is in the function call and then binds the function definition with the newly created definition.

Question #131

When is a class template instantiated?

Answer

Class templates are instantiated when we create an object using the template argument, as shown in the following example:

```
template <class T>
class Sample
{
    // code for the class
};
void main()
{
    Sample <int> obj1;
    Sample <float> obj2;
    Sample <double> obj3;
};
```

When *obj1*, *obj2* and *obj3* objects are instantiated (created), the class template is instantiated for each type and hence three different versions of the class template are created.

Question #132

Write a function template that swaps the values of two variables of any primitive data type.

Answer

```
template <class T>
void swap(T x, T y)
{
    T temp;
    temp = x;
    x = y;
    y = temp;
}
```

Question #133

What is the STL?

Answer

Standard Template Library (STL) is a C++ library of container classes (along with algorithms that manipulate the data stored in containers) and iterators (that are used to move thought the elements of the containers).

Every container in the STL is a template. The purpose of the containers classes is to contain their objects. Examples of containers are *list*, *vector*, and *map*.

You can, for example, use a *vector<int>* in much the same way as you would use an ordinary C/C++ array, except, that vector eliminates the chore of managing dynamic memory allocation by hand.

Question #134

What is a stream?

Answer

A stream basically is a sequence of bytes. It can either act as a *source* from which the program can take (extract) input data or as a *destination* to which the program can send (insert) output data.

The source stream that supplies data to the program is called *input stream* and the destination stream that receives data from the program is called *output stream*. These streams collectively are called *data streams*.

Question #135

What are the benefits of using streams?

Answer

The C++ I/O subsystem is designed to work with a wide variety of devices that includes keyboard, monitor, disks, tape drives, etc. The working principle (characteristics) of each of these devices is quite different. The C++ I/O subsystem is designed in such a way that it provides a uniform interface that is independent of the actual device being used. Thus, the programmer can write a C++ program that can receive input from, and send output to any device without bothering about the characteristics of device being used. This interface is called a *stream*.

Question #136

What are pre-defined console streams in C++?

Answer

When a C++ program begins execution, the following console streams are automatically opened and are closed when the program finished execution:

- The first one, known as the *standard input stream*, represented by an object *cin* of *istream* class, is the stream from which input is received. This stream usually receives input from keyboard, but using redirection, the stream can obtain input from a disk file or another input device.
- The second one, known as *standard output stream*, represented by an object *cout* of *ostream* class, is the stream to which output is sent. The stream usually sends output to computer screen, but using redirection, the stream can send output to a disk file or to another output device.
- The third one, known as *standard error stream*, represented by an object *cerr* of *ostream* class, is the stream to which error messages are sent. This stream always sends error messages to computer screen. The redirection does not work for this stream. Therefore, even if you use redirection, the output of the program will be send to the specified disk file or device, the error messages, if any, continue to appear on computer screen.

Question #137

What are the limitations of reading data using overloaded extraction operator '>>'?

Answer

- The use of comma as a separator is not permitted.
- It can read only non-white space characters.
- It cannot read multiword strings as these strings use embedded space character which will be interpreted as value terminating character.

Question #138

What are the default setting for the output using the overloaded insertion '<<' operator?

Answer

The default settings for the output are as follows:

- Values are always displays from left to right character by character.
- The columns used to print a value are always equal to the number of characters of that particular item.
- The trailing zeros in the fractional part of a real number are not displayed. If the fractional part is zero, then the decimal point is also not displayed.

Question #139

What are the features supported by C++ I/O subsystem that can be used to format the output?

Answer

If you want to control the output in your own way, you have to use formatted output operations. The C++ I/O subsystem provides a number of features that can be used to format the output as desired.

These features include:

- *ios* class functions and flags.
- Predefined Manipulators.
- User-defined manipulators.

Question #140

What are manipulators?

Answer

Manipulators are special functions that are designed to modify the working of streams. These are defined in *iomanip.h* header file. Various manipulators are categorized into following two types:

- Non-parameterized Manipulators – manipulators that take an argument.
- Parameterized Manipulators – manipulators that take no argument.

Question #141

Given a choice which one you will prefer to use manipulators or member functions of *ios* class?

Answer

I will prefer to use manipulators. The reason being that on one side they provide the same features as those of member functions of *ios* class, and on the other side they are more convenient to use. They don't need an object to invoke them as in the case of *ios* member function that can only be invoked on an object of output stream. Further they can be cascaded.

Question #142

Can we design our own manipulators?

Answer

We can design our own manipulators, called user-defined manipulators, to control the output in a certain manner.

Question #143

In what different ways a file can be opened?

Answer

For opening a file, first we have to create a file stream and then link it with the file. A file stream can be created using the class *ifstream*, *ofstream*, and *fstream* that are defined in *fstream.h* header file. The actual class to be used depends upon the purpose, *i.e.*, whether we want to read data from the file or write data to the file or we want to read from and write to the same file. A file can be opened in two ways:

- Using constructor of the appropriate file stream class.
- Using *open()* member function of the appropriate file stream class.

Question #144

How can a file be opened using a constrictor of an appropriate class?

Answer

We know that a constructor is used to initialize an object while it is being created. Here, filename is used as an argument for the constructor, which is then used to initialize the file stream object.

Prototype of generalized constructor of *ifstream* class is

```
ifstream(const char *path,int mode=ios::in,int prot=filebuf::openprot);
```

Prototype of generalized constructor of *ofstream* class is

```
ofstream(const char *path,int mode=ios::out,int prot=filebuf::openprot);
```

Prototype of generalized constructor of *fstream* class is

```
fstream(const char *path,int mode=ios::in|ios::out,int prot=filebuf::openprot);
```

where *path* is filename with path information, however, if path information is omitted, file is considered to be in the working directory; *mode* is file opening mode, default argument with default value 'in' and 'out' for input-output mode; *prot* is access specifier, default argument with default value 'openprot' for read and write access permissions.

Question #145

How can a file be opened using *open*() member function?

Answer

The prototype of *open()* function is

```
void open(const char *path,int mode,int prot = filebuf::openprot);
```

where *path* is filename with path information, however, if path information is omitted, file is considered to be in the working directory; *mode* is file opening mode; *prot* is access specifier, default argument with default value 'openprot' for read and write access permissions.

The *open()* function is invoked on a file stream object as

```
file-stream-object.open("filename", mode );
```

Question #146

What are various error handling functions that can be used to for safe file handling?

Answer

Various error handling functions that can be used to for safe file handling is listed below:

Table 6.7: Error handling functions

Function	Purpose
eof()	Return non-zero (true) value if end-of-file (EOF) encountered while reading a file, otherwise returns zero (false) value.
fail()	Return non-zero (true) value if open, read, or write operations has failed; otherwise returns zero (false) value to indicate success of operation.
bad()	Return non-zero (true) value if invalid operation is attempted or any media (unrecoverable) error occurs; otherwise returns zero (false) value.
good()	Return non-zero (true) value every thing is fine; otherwise returns zero (false) value.
rdstate()	Returns the value of the state data member of ios class.
clear()	Clear the current error state so that further operations can be attempted.

Question #147

What is the *mutable* keyword? When do you use it?

Answer

The presence of the *mutable* keyword indicates that the data member of a class may be safely changed within a *const* member function. Mutable could be used as workaround solution for a design bug.

```
class A
{
    private:
        int i;
        mutable int j;
    public :
        void get() const
        {
            i = 20:     // Not allowed
            j = 30;     // Allowed
        }
};
```

Question #148

What is the difference between overloading and overriding?

Answer

Overloading a method (or function) is the ability for methods of the same name to be re-defined as long as these methods have different signatures (different set of parameters).

Method overriding is the ability of the inherited class rewriting the virtual method of the base class.

Question #149

What is the casting?

Answer

If a class is derived from a base class containing virtual functions, a pointer to that base class type can be used to call the implementations of the virtual functions residing in the derived class object. Since a derived class completely contains the definitions of all the base classes from which it is derived, it is safe to cast a pointer up the class hierarchy to any of these base classes.

Question #150

What is the RTTI?

Answer

Run-Time Type Identification (RTTI) mechanism is used to determine the exact type of an object pointer or reference during runtime of a program, *i.e.*, it identifies whether the base class pointer holds the address of a base class object or a subclass object.

Operator *typeid* retrieves the runtime information association with a certain object *typeid* takes an object or a type name as its argument. Thus, to determine if the dynamic type of object *x* is of class *Y*, check whether the expression *typeid(x)* = = *typeid (Y)* is true.

❑ ❑ ❑

Chapter 7

The Java Language

Question #1

Java is not just another programming language; it is a technology in itself. Do you agree with the statement? If yes, justify.

Answer

Yes, Java is a technology comprising of the following:

- ***Programming language*** - The syntax of Java programming is similar to C++ syntax. You can use Java programming language to create all kinds of applications that you could create using any language such as C++.

- ***Development environment*** - Java programming language is usually mentioned in the context of the World Wide Web (WWW) and browsers that are capable of running programs called *applets*. Applets are very small size programs written in Java programming language that resides on the WWW servers, are downloaded by a browser to a client's system, and run by that browser. The size of the applets is kept small in order to minimize the download time. Applets are invoked through web pages written in HyperText Markup Language (HTML).

As a development environment, Java technology provides a large suite of tools that a programmer can use to develop applications. These tools include a compiler (*javac*), an interpreter (*java*), a document generator (*javadoc*), debugger (*jdb*), and so on.

- ***Application environment*** - Java applications are standalone programs that do not require a Web browser to execute. These are typically general-purpose programs that can run on any system where the Java Runtime Environment (JRE) is installed.

- ***Deployment environment*** - There are two main deployment environments for Java programs. In first deployment environment, JRE supplied by the Java 2 Software Development Kit (SDK) contains the complete set of class files for all the Java packages, which includes basic language classes, Graphical User Interface (GUI) component classes, advanced collections Application Programming Interface (API), and so on. The second deployment environment is the Web browser. Most commercial Web browsers supply a Java interpreter and runtime environment.

Question #2

What is the name of the project under which development of Java begun? Who was the project leader? What was the original name of Java language? When was it changed to Java? Is there was a technical reason for its change of name?

Answer

The name of the project was *Green*. James Gosling was the project leader. The original name of Java language was *Oak*. Its name was changed in the year 1995. No, there was no technical reason; it was just for marketing and legal reasons, when it was introduced at *SunWorld'95*.

Question #3

What are different flavours of Java language?

Answer

Java language is the only language available in three different flavours to suit the requirements of different environments:

- ***Standard edition (Core Java)*** – This edition meets the requirements of applets and standard application. The development kit is named as J2SDK.
- ***Enterprise edition*** – This edition (which is collection many Java technologies such as JSP, EJB, etc.) meets the requirements of larger organizations (enterprise). The development kit is named as J2EE.
- ***Micro edition*** – This edition meets the requirements of mobiles and other portable devices. The development kit is named as J2ME.

Question #4

What are the key features of Java language? OR List key features of Java language.

Answer

The key features of Java language are:

- Simple
- Object Oriented
- Robust
- Distributed
- Secure
- Architecture-Neutral
- Portable
- Interpreted
- High Performance
- Multithreaded
- Dynamic

Question #5

When we say Java is robust, what does it mean?

Answer

When we say robust, it means which rarely fails. The Java language is designed for creating highly *reliable* software. It provides extensive compile-time checking, followed by a second level of run-time checking. The errors are detected very early in the development phases which are shown up at run-time in other languages. Being strictly typed, it checks the code at compile time and also checks the code at run time.

Question #6

When we say Java is secure, what does it mean?

Answer

When we say secure, it means that execution of a program in Java environment is safe and does not pose any security threat (breach).

The Java applets that accompany the web pages are not allowed to access local file system, thus Java run time environment acts as a firewall between a networked application and user's computer.

Question #7

When we say Java is platform-independent (architectural-neutral), what does it mean?

Answer

It means that a Java program can be run on any computer running any OS provided JVM is installed on that system.

Question #8

How Java achieves platform-independence?

Answer

It achieves platform-independence through *bytecode*, which is an intermediate code.

Each Java program is converted into one or more class files. The content of the class file is a set of instructions called *bytecode* to be executed by JVM.

Question #9

When we say Java is dynamic, what does it mean?

Answer

Dynamic, usually, refers to what is happening at execution time. To execute a Java application, not all the classes (comprising an application) are loaded before starting the execution of the Java application.

Rather, Java runtime environment determines a minimum set of classes to start the application and the other classes are loaded as and when they are required.

Question #10

When we say Java is distributed, what does it mean?

Answer

By distributed, we mean that various classes making up the complete application can be stored at different computers (which can be at distant geographic locations0 across the network.

Whenever, there is a reference to remote class during the execution of Java application, the referenced class is downloaded from the remote computer.

Question #11

When we say Java is multithreaded, what does it mean?

Answer

It means that Java provides support for multithreaded environment which allows us to write programs that can do many things simultaneously. Java is very well suited to write high performance programs especially for server-side development.

Question #12

What is a Java Virtual Machine (JVM)?

Answer

The *Java Virtual Machine Specification* defines JVM as follows:

> *"An imaginary machine that is implemented by emulating it in software on a real machine. Code for the Java virtual machine is stored in .class files, each of which contains code for at most one public class."*

The JVM specification provides the hardware platform specification to which all Java technology code is compiled. This specification enables Java software to be platform independent because the compilation is done for a generic machine known as the Java Virtual Machine (JVM). You can emulate this generic machine in software to run on various existing computer systems or implement in hardware.

Java compiler takes the Java application source code and generates bytecode. Bytecode consist of instructions for the JVM. Every Java interpreter, regardless of whether it is a Java technology development tool or a Web browser that can run applets, has an implementation of the JVM.

Question #13

What is the bytecode?

Answer

Each Java program is converted into one or more class files. The content of the class file is a set of instructions called bytecode to be executed by Java virtual machine (JVM). JMV is an interpreter for bytecode. Java introduces bytecode to create platform (hardware) independent program.

Question #14

What is the Just-In-Time (JIT) compiler?

Answer

The Java interpreter on any platform will interpret the compiled bytecode into instructions understandable by the particular hardware. However, the Java virtual machine handles one bytecode instruction at a time. The Java Just-In-Time compiler compiles the bytecode into the particular machine code (as though the program had been compiled initially on that platform). Once the code has been (re-) compiled by the JIT compiler, it will usually run more quickly in that system.

Question #15

Enumerate the differences between C++ and Java

Answer

Table 7.1: Differences between C++ and Java

C++	Java
Data types may take variable length, i.e., number of bytes/words used may vary.	Data types fixed length, i.e., uses fixed number of bits for a particular data type irrespective of the underlying platform.
Data members cannot be initialized in class definition.	Data members can be initialized in class definition.
If variables and data members are not initialized explicitly, they take garbage values (undefined value).	If variables and data members are not initialized explicitly, they take default values.
Support implicit type conversion.	Doesn't support implicit type conversion.
Support pointers.	Doesn't support pointers.
Support operator overloading.	Doesn't support operator overloading.
Support multiple class inheritance.	Doesn't support multiple class inheritance. However, it supports multiple inheritance using interfaces.
Support global variables, global functions, typedefs, structures, and unions.	Doesn't support global variables, global functions, typedef, structures or unions.
Support default arguments for a function.	Doesn't support default arguments for a function.

Table 7.1: Differences between C++ and Java *Contd.*

Support templates.	Doesn't support templates.
Support friend functions.	Doesn't support friend functions.
Support destructors to perform the clean up task.	Doesn't support destructors. However, the finalize method performs the task equivalent to that of destructor.
Doesn't have the concept of packages and interfaces.	Support the concept of packages and interfaces.
Doesn't provide support for multithreading.	Provide support for multithreading.
Doesn't support automatic garbage collection. Releasing the memory is developer's responsibility.	Support automatic garbage collection, and thus frees the developer from the hackles of having to manage memory.
There is no way to prohibit a class or member function from being overridden.	Uses *final* keyword to prohibit a class or method to be overridden.

Question #16

Is there any restriction on the name of the Java source file?

Answer

Yes. The name of the file must match the name of the class containing main method.

Question #17

Why does the main method need a *static* modifier?

Answer

Because static methods and members don't need an instance of their class to invoke them and main is the first method which is invoked.

Question #18

Will the program compile, if the main method doesn't have static modifier?

Answer

Yes, it will compile, but the program will not execute.

Question #19

The main method is usually defined in a public class as

```
public static void main(String args[]) {
    // code
}
```

Can we interchange the *public* and *static* keywords?

Answer

Yes. As a standard convention, it should be avoided.

Question #20

Which is the default parent class for a Java class?

Answer

The *Object* class (defined in *java.lang* package) by default (implicit) is parent class of all the classes unless they have their own parent class. Also, the package *java.lang* is imported into all Java files by default.

Question #21

How arguments are passed to a method in Java?

Answer

In Java, arguments, primitive as well as objects, are *passed by value*. When an object passed as argument, the object's reference will be copied.

Question #22

What are *native* methods?

Answer

Native methods are methods implemented in another programming language such as C. The Java Native Interface (JNI) is the API to invoke these native methods from a Java class.

Question #23

List the main differences between an applet and an application.

Answer

Applets are useful for creating dynamic and interactive web applications. An applet runs under the control of a browser, where as an application runs as a stand alone application on the desktop.

An applet is subjected to tougher security restrictions in terms of file and network access, whereas an application can easily access the file system and network.

Question #24

Are there any keywords that are reserved?

Answer

Yes, the keywords *goto* and *const* are reserved in Java. By reserved means that at present they are not being used, but are kept with a hope that they may find their use in future.

Question #25

What are the default values for variables, fields (data members) of data types and reference types?

Answer

There is nothing like a garbage value or undefined value as is in C/C++ languages. Each variable or field takes default value as shown value assigned depend the type of the field.

Table 7.2: Default initial values for fields

Variable Type	Default Value
byte	0
short	0
int	0
long	0*L* (0*l*)
float	0.0*F* (0.0*f*)
double	0.0*D* (0.0*d*)
char	'\u0000'
boolean	false
All types of references	null

Question #26

What is the use of *this* and *super*?

Answer

The *this* keyword is used to refer to the current object instance.

The *super* keyword is used to refer to the variables and methods of the *superclass* of the current object instance's class.

Question #27

Explain the role of access specifiers (*public*, *private*, *protected*, *default*) for a class, a method, and a variable.

Answer

public **Access Specifier:** A class that is declared as *public* has global scope and an instance of this class can be created from any where within or outside of the class, *i.e.*, by other classes in the same package as well as classes in other packages. Only one non-inner class in any file can be defined with the *public* keyword. The *public* modifier can be used for variables, methods and classes.

protected **Access Specifier:** A protected variable is visible within the same class, same package and in subclasses in other packages. Any class in the same directory is considered to be in the default package, and thus protected classes will be visible. This can be used for methods, variables and inner classes.

private **Access Specifier:** Private variables are only visible from within the same class. This means they are not visible within sub classes. This allows a variable to be insulated from being modified by any methods except those in the current class. This can only be used for methods, variables and inner classes.

***default* Access Specifier:** A variable defined with no access modifier is said to have default visibility. Default visibility means a variables/method can be seen within the class and from elsewhere within the same package, but not from other packages.

Question #28

What are the widening and narrowing conversions?

Answer

When we cast an object of lesser size to an object of larger size, it is a widening conversion, *e.g.*, *int* to *long*. When we cast an object of larger size to an object of lesser size, it is a narrowing conversion, *e.g.*, *int* to *long*.

Question #29

How can we create Java API documentation?

Answer

This can be done using the *Javadoc* tool. It parses the declarations and documentation comments in a set of Java source files and produces a corresponding set of HTML pages describing (by default) the public and protected classes, nested classes (but not anonymous inner classes), interfaces, constructors, methods and fields.

We can use it to generate the API (Application Programming Interface) documentation or the implementation documentation for a set of source files.

Question #30

What is a garbage collection?

Answer

Note that when an object is no longer required, its memory needs to be cleaned up and freed. Garbage collection is the automatic collection of non-active objects. This task is done by the *garbage collector* which is a thread running as part of the JVM process.

Question #31

Can the garbage collector be forced to run invoking it explicitly?

Answer

No. Though, we can make an explicit call to garbage collector as *system.gc()*, it only suggests that the JVM must extend effort toward recycling unused objects in order to make the memory they currently occupy available for reuse. When the control returns from the call, the JVM has made a best effort to reclaim space from all discarded objects. This doesn't guarantee that the garbage collector is called.

Question #32

What is t he difference between a *String* and *StringBuffer* class?

Answer

String class is immutable, *i.e.*, it cannot be modified once declared.

StringBuffer class is not immutable and strings can be appended to the original string. It is more efficient than using *String* when the string value could be changed.

Question #33

What is the use of *StringTokenizer* class?

Answer

The *StringTokenizer* class breaks a string into tokens.

The following code

```
StringTokenizer str = new StringTokenizer("Tic Tic Toe");

while ( st.hasmoretokens() )
{
    System.out.printin( st.nexttoken() );
}
```

produces following output:

```
Tic
Tic
Toe
```

Question #34

What are different ways to create a thread?

Answer

There are two ways to create a thread, each one is described below:

- By creating a new class that extends *Thread* class. This should be done only if the new class is not extending another class.

```
public class Counter extends Thread {
    // code for new class
    public void run() {
        // code goes here . . .
    }
}
```

The above example creates a new class *Counter* that extends the *Thread* class and overrides the *run()* method of the *Thread* class. The *run()* method is where all the work of the *Counter* class thread is done.

- By creating a new class that implements *Runnable* interface.

```
public class Counter implements Runnable {
    Threads t;
    public void run() {
        // code goes here . . .
    }
}
```

Here, the abstract *run()* method is defined in the *Runnable* interface and is being implemented. Note that we have an instance of the *Thread* class as a variable of the *Counter* class.

Question #35

Which way of creating a thread is more flexible?

Answer

Method of creating a class by implementing *Runnable*, is more flexible because there is an still a scope of extending a class.

If a thread is created by extending *Thread* class, then new class cannot extend another class.

Question #36

How the newly created thread is started?

Answer

The newly created thread is started by invoking *start()* method of the *Thread* class. The *start()* method creates the system resources necessary to run the thread and schedules the thread to run. After the *start()* method has returned, the thread is actually in the runnable state. When a thread gets the CPU time, it will be executed.

Question #37

How is a thread prioritized?

Answer

Execution of multiple threads on a single CPU, in some order, is called *scheduling*. The Java runtime supports a very simple, deterministic scheduling algorithm known as *fixed priority scheduling*. This algorithm schedules threads based on their priority relative to other runnable threads.

When a Java thread is created, it inherits its priority from the thread that created it. You can also modify a threads priority at any time after its creation using the *setPriority()* method.

Thread priorities are integers ranging between MIN_PRIORITY(1) and MAX_PRIORITY (10) (constants defined in the *Thread* class). The value 5 is the default priority.

The higher the integer, the higher the priority. At any given time, when multiple threads are ready to be executed, the runtime system chooses the runnable thread with the highest priority for execution. Only when that threads stops, yields or becomes not runnable for some reasons will a lower priority thread start executing. If two threads of the same priority are waiting for the CPU, the scheduler chooses one of them to run in a round-robin fashion. The chosen thread will run until one of the following conditions is true:

- A higher priority thread becomes runnable.
- It yields, or its run method exits.
- On systems that support time-slicing, its time allotment has expired.

Then, the second thread is given a chance to run and so on, until the interpreter exits.

The Java runtime system's thread scheduling algorithm is also pre-emptive. If at any time a thread with a higher priority than all other runnable threads becomes runnable, the runtime system chooses the new higher priority thread for execution. Then new higher priority thread is said to preempt the other threads.

Question #38

How yielding is different from sleeping in threads?

Answer

Yielding means when a thread invokes its *yield()* method, it returns to the ready state.

Sleeping means when a thread invokes its *sleep()* method, it returns to the waiting state.

Question #39

How pre-emptive scheduling is different from time-slicing?

Answer

Under pre-emptive scheduling, the highest priority thread executes until it enters the waiting or dead states or a higher priority thread comes into existence.

Under time-slicing, a thread executes for a pre-defined slice of time and then re-enters the pool of ready threads. The scheduler then determines which thread should execute next, based on priority and other factors.

Question # 40

What are synchronized statements and methods?

Answer

A synchronized statement can only be executed after a thread has acquired the lock for the object or class referenced in the synchronized statement. This means that no other thread can access the object till the current thread releases the object. This is used to make code thread safe and prevent dirty reads.

Synchronized methods are methods that are used to control access to an object. A thread only executes a synchronized method after it has acquired the lock for the method's object or class.

Synchronized methods are similar to synchronized statements.

Question #41

When do we need to use synchronized statements?

Answer

We need to use synchronized in following circumstances:

- When we wish to synchronize only a part of the method.

```
void myMmethod() {
    // some statementx
    synchronized(this) {
       this.a = 20;
    }
    // more statements
}
```

- When a class whose object to be locked is part of a third party jar file.

```
void myMethod() {
    // some statement
    synchronized(thirdPartyObject) {
        ThirdPartyObject.a = 20;
    }
    // more statements
}
```

Question #42

Can we restart a dead thread?

Answer

No, a dead thread cannot be restarted.

Question #43

When a thread's *run()* method is invoked?

Answer

Whenever, the scheduler schedules (selects) thread for execution, it thread's *run()* method.

Question #44

When do threads leave the runnable state?

Answer

A thread leaves the runnable state when one of the following events occurs:

- Its sleep method is invoked
- The thread calls the wait method to wait for a specific condition to be satisfied.
- The thread is blocking on I/O.

Question #45

What is a monitor?

Answer

A monitor is lock on an object which allows only one thread to gain access to the underlying object.

Question #46

How can you make code thread safe?

Answer

By using *synchronized* keyword. It marks a block of code or an entire method as a *critical section.* Only one thread can execute it at any point in time. Other threads will have to wait for their turn to use the critical section.

When an instance method is synchronized, the synchronized code can be run by many threads on different objects simultaneously, since the locking is on the object.

For a synchronized class method, the locking is on the class object, which thus limits to only one thread executing that code.

Question #47

What is a daemon thread?

Answer

Daemon threads are sometime called *service* threads that normally run at a low priority and provide a basic service to a program(s) when activity on a machine is reduced.

The garbage collector thread is an example of a daemon thread. This thread, provided by the JVM, will scan programs for variables/references that go out of scope and free up their resources back to the system. A thread can set the daemon flag by passing a true boolean value to the *setDaemon()* method. If a false boolean value is passed, the thread will become a user thread. However, this must occur before the thread has been started.

The JVM scheduler's basic rule is that if there are only daemon threads running, the JVM will exit (terminate).

Question #48

What are checked and unchecked exceptions?

Answer

Checked Exceptions

- They represent invalid condition in areas outside the immediate control of the program such as valid user input, database problems, network outages, missing files, etc.
- They are subclasses of *Exception* class.
- Their methods are *obliged* to establish a policy for all checked exception thrown by its implementation (either pass the checked exception further up the stack, or handle it somehow).

Unchecked Exceptions

- They represent defects in the program such invalid arguments passed to a non-private method.
- They are subclasses of *RuntimeException*, and are usually implemented using *IllegalArgumentException*, *NullPointerException*, or *IllegalStateException.*
- Their methods are *not obliged* to establish a policy for the unchecked exceptions thrown by its implementation (and they almost always do not do so).

Question #49

What is a *Throwable* class?

Answer

It is a super class of all errors and exceptions classes in the Java language. Only objects that are instances of this class (or one of its subclasses) are thrown by the JVM or can be thrown by the Java *throw* statement. Similarly, only this class or one of its sub classes can be the argument type in a catch clause.

Question #50

What is the order of execution of *try, catch, finally*? What happens if an exception occurs in the *finally* block?

Answer

```
try {
   // statements which may throw an exception
} catch(execeptionType1 identifier1) {
   // statements to handle exception
}
catch(exceptionType2 identifier2) {
   // statements to handle exception
}
finally {
   // statements to handle exception
}
```

- Every try block must have either one catch clause or a finally clause.
- We can have multiple catch clauses but only one finally clause.
- The statements within the try block are executed until an exception is thrown or it completes successfully.
- We get a compiler-error if the code included in the try statement will never throw one of the caught checked executions.
- If an exception is thrown, each catch clause is inspected in turn for a type to which the exception can be assigned.
- The catch blocks must be ordered from most specific to least specific. For example, the *catch(Exception e)* should come last after all the other exceptions like *catch(IOException e)*.
- When a match is found, the exception object is assigned to the identifier and the statements catch block are executed.
- A catch clause may throw another exception.
- If a finally clause is included, its statements are executed after all other try-catch processing is complete.
- The finally clause executes whether or not an exception is thrown or a break or continue are encountered.
- If a catch clause invokes *System.exit()*, the finally clause will not execute.

Question #51

Can you create you create your own exceptions?

Answer

Yes. Any new exception can be created by extending the *Exception* class. You are required to override the *toString()* method to print an appropriate error message.

Question #52

What happens if an exception is not caught?

Answer

When an exception is not caught, the *uncaughtException()* method of the thread's *ThreadGroup* is invoked, which terminates the program in which it is thrown.

Question #53

What are the characteristics of *final*, *finally* keywords and *finalize* method?

Answer

The *final* Keyword

- When a variable is marked as final, then the compiler could perform various optimizations knowing that its value cannot change.
- Class member variables can be declared as final without a value assigned to it. This forces all its constructors to initialize the blank final variables.
- When a static variable declared as final, it is similar to constant variable of C language when a class declared as final, it can't be sub-classed
- If an object or array (array in Java is an object) is declared as *final*, it does not stop you from changing in the fields in the object or elements of the array. It just stops you from

pointing that variable to a different object or array. If you want to protect the object, you must make it *immutable*.

- When a method declared as final, it can't be overridden.

The *finally* Keyword

It is use in exception handling. The finally block is placed after a try catch block. The code contained in the finally block would get executed under following conditions;

- If exception is thrown in try block
- If exception is not thrown in try block
- If exception is thrown in catch block
- We usually close resources or clean up variables inside the finally block. See the example below

```
class X {
    void dbupdate() {
        Connection connection = new Connection(. . .);
        try {
            doSomeUpdates();    // using connection instance
        }
        catch(DatabaseException e) {
            System.out.printin("The error is " + e.toString());
            throw e;
        }
        finally {
            connection.close();    //always executed
        }
}
```

In this example, *connection* instance is getting closed inside the *finally* as it is safer approach.

The *finalize* Method

It is used for garbage collection. You can put clean up code in the finalize method. When an object is about to be garbage collected, its finalize method will run.

Question #54

How are *this()* and *super()* methods used with constructors?

Answer

The *this()* method within a constructor is used to invoke another constructor in the same class.

The *super()* method within a constructor is used to invoke its immediate super class constructor.

Question #55

What is the *overloading* and *overriding* of methods?

Answer

Polymorphism refers to the ability of a method to behave differently based on the kind of input.

There are two ways in which polymorphism is implemented in Java:

- Overloading
- Overriding

Overloading Methods

Overloaded methods have same name, but different parameter lists (signature) and returns types and appears in the same class or subclass. The decision as to which method should be called is taken at runtime, based on the parameter list. This is known as *late-binding*.

An example of an overloaded method is *abs()* in the *Java.lang.Math* class

```
public static double abs(double a)
public static float abs(float a)
public static int abs(int a)
public static long abs(long a)
```

Overriding Methods

In overriding, we *re-define* a method that is inherited from a super class.

- Overridden methods can only exist in subclasses. They have the same name and method signature.
- The access modifier for the overriding method may not be more restrictive than the access modifier of the supper class method.
- Private methods are not inherited so we can have any access modifier in subclass.
- The throws clause of the overriding method may only include exceptions that are thrown by the super class method, including it's subclasses.

Question #56

Compare and contrast between an *interface* and an *abstract class.*

Answer

- Neither interface nor abstract classes can be instantiated.
- Direct multiple inheritance is not supported in Java, like in C++. The interfaces take care of this aspect. A class can implement any number of interfaces, but can extend only one class.
- An interface has all public members and no implementation. An Abstract class is a class which may have the usual flavors of class members (private, protected, etc.), but has some abstract methods.
- Use interface as much as possible and only use an abstract class in the case where you want to provide some (but not all, of course) implementation.

Question #57

What is the object serialization?

Answer

Serialization refers to the process of writing the contents of an object to a file and re-creating the object from the file later.

Question #58

Compare and contrast between *byte streams* and *character streams.*

Answer

Byte Streams	Character Streams
java.io.InputStream and java.io.OutputStream are the base byte stream classes. These are 8 bit streams.	*java.io.Reader* and *java.io.Writer* are the base character streams. These are 16-bit unicode character streams.
The method names end with a suffix *InputStream* or *OutputStream.*	The method names end with a suffix *Reader* or *Writer*.
They are less efficient.	They are more efficient.

Question #59

What are the types of variables that can be there in an interface?

Answer

An interface is like a class but with a few restrictions.

1. All its variables must be static final, *i.e.*, constants.
2. A class can inherit multiple interfaces.
3. All methods in an interface are implicitly declared public and abstract.
4. All variables in an interface must be constants. They are implicitly declared public static final.

Question #60

What are wrapper classes?

Answer

Note that primitive values in Java are not objects. In order to manipulate these values as objects, a wrapper class, declared as final, is provided for each primitive type. The objects of all wrapper classes are immutable, i.e., their state cannot be changed.

Table 7.3: Primitive and corresponding wrapper class

Type	Wrapper Class	Type	Wrapper Class
byte	Byte	float	Float
short	Short	double	Double
int	Integer	boolean	Boolean
long	Long	char	Character

Example:

```
Integer intObj = new Integer(200);
```

It construct an integer object named *intObj* from integer literal 200.

Question #61

List the important classes contained in *java.lang* package?

Answer

Note that *java.lang* package is indispensable when programming in Java. It is automatically imported into every Java source file at compile time.
The prominent classes contained in this package are include

- *Object* class, which is mother of all classes.
- Wrapper classes (*Character*, *Byte*, *Short*, *Integer*, *Long*, *Float*, *Double*, *Boolean*), for handling primitive values as objects.
- *Thread* class, for dealing with threads.
- *Throwable* class, for handling exceptions.
- *Math* class, for dealing with mathematical functions.
- *String* and *StringBuffer* classes, for dealing with strings.

❑ ❑ ❑